BRITISH MUSLIMS EXPECTATIONS OF THE GOVERNMENT

SECULAR OR ISLAMIC? WHAT SCHOOLS DO BRITISH MUSLIMS WANT FOR THEIR CHILDREN?

SAIED R. AMELI
ALIYA AZAM
ARZU MERALI

Islamic Human Rights Commission
www.ihrc.org.uk

2005

PUBLISHED BY ISLAMIC HUMAN RIGHTS COMMISSION

First published in Great Britain in 2005
by Islamic Human Rights Commission
PO Box 598, Wembley, HA9 7XH

© 2005 Islamic Human Rights Commission

Printed in England by Islamic Human Rights Commission
Design & Typeset: Ibrahim Sadikovic
Printed by Impeks Litho Ltd

ISBN 1-903718-27-9

CONTENTS

LIST OF FIGURES AND TABLES

ACKNOWLEDGEMENTS

IHRC would like to thank the following for their support and critical contributions towards the completion of this volume:

Hiba Abdul-Rahim, Ali Abidi, Aliya Abidi, Fatima Abidi, Samana Abidi, Abbas Ameli, Fahad Ansari, Mahum Hashim, Huda Hlaiyil, Soheila Hojeij, Anam Hussain, Rashidul Islam, Nazia Kalsoom, Seyfeddin Kara, Raza Kazim, Zohra Khaku, Fatema Khoei, Seerat Fatema, Senar Madali, Abidah Merchant, Ali Reza Moafi, Massoud Shadjareh, Zainab Shadjareh and Rianne C. ven Teen.

We would like to once more thank the Joseph Rowntree Charitable Trust and the other supporters of IHRC for their continued support of the British Muslims' Expectations of the Government project.

We are also grateful for the important insights and critical review of Dr. Shaikh Abdul Mabud, as well as the discerning contributions of Jamila Fernandez and Ibrahim Hewitt. Our thanks also to Amina Al-Yassine, Riyaz Daya, Changez Ali Khan and Hajirah Qureishi for the wisdom that youth brings.

Special acknowledgements and thanks from Aliya Azam as well as the IHRC team to her children Maliha, Haider, Ali Akbar and Jafar Azam.

FOREWORD

Education as a human right is something that many take for granted as being an actual and aspirational legitimacy, and one that is universally provided for in the United Kingdom. However, educational choice, the nature and diversity of education and provision of minority education have become pariahs in the discourse surrounding education and development of grounded and inclusive citizenship in recent times.

Faith schooling is demonised as divisive and the provision of faith-friendly facilities at school as favouring minorities to the detriment of their peers. Sadly, such views are not the sole provenance of the tabloid and right wing press but cut across policy makers and commentators from all parts of the political spectrum. Yet the right to minority education, and the rights of parents to choose the type of their child's education are enshrined in international documents and norms, and all arguments to the contrary do not simply disregard those, norms, but are prone to emulate or create the atmosphere of division, hatred and violence that those international norms were created to move away from. Put simply, the role of education in the interwar years and throughout the Nazi era in Europe habituated majority populations to the idea that those unlike them were not equal to them.

This process was not nearly as crude as many may think, but the result of the institutionalisation of deeply held prejudices that operated at systemic levels within education systems to the detriment of minority pupils. This detriment eventuated into violence, perpetrated not by the minority but by the majority. Characteristics of that process of systemisation was the invocation at policy level of the rights, importance and singularity of nation as defined by the elite and democratically elected legislatures of those nations. In other words, monocentric and ideologically rigid education systems necessarily violate the principles of individual, minority and ultimately societal human rights.

Set in the on-going context of vigorous discussion about inclusive citizenship, this volume seeks to tease out Muslim expectations of the British government regarding education and how these expectations supply the clues and even models for a genuinely rights based, egalitarian education system, where inclusivity and equality have actual meaning for all concerned.

In a climate where fear of the other and their presumed inherent potential for violence exist, it is worth remembering that historically in Europe these presuppositions led to extreme violence against the minorities from whence threat was perceived and not vice-versa.

Islamic Human Rights Commission

INTRODUCTION

Current debates regarding religion in the public sphere have tended to be characterised by a secular-minded media and political elite as the statements of reason and egalitarianism, positing faith in the role of a (potentially) divisive and disruptive factor in social life, whose influence needs to be minimised and consigned to a private sphere. Whilst in most facets of society this may well already be the case, an area of resurgent interest and existing political space for religion is within British education. This revised interest is marked out by the phenomenal growth in faith schooling, particularly Muslim faith schooling, in an educational space with a long history of faith schools. It is also seen in the very public battles over religious expression – notably Islamic dress for girls – fought in the law courts, as well as in the negative comments of government officials and social commentators which seem to imply faith identity as inimical to good citizenship.

Faith schools are implied to be, and often explicitly stated by their detractors as being social spaces that undermine social cohesion – and Muslim schools in particular have come under fire in a climate where hostility against Muslims is becoming commonplace. The facilitation of religious practice, whether through instruction or dress code etc., in school, has also come under fire particularly after France banned the wearing of hijab in schools and other European countries indicating that they may follow suit. Ironically, rather than promoting egalitarianism, this tack flies in the face of the Universal Declaration of Human Rights (1948), article 26.3 of which states that *'Parents have a prior right to choose the kind of education that shall be given to their children.'*

In this light, this research looks at the negative perceptions of religion, Islam and faith schooling and assesses its impact on Muslim parents and students through quantitative and qualitative research. Whilst asserting parental rights in the context of international norms at the outset, this report also seeks to tease out the positive implications of these rights, not simply as a tool to promote the desires of parents of minority faith communities, but as part of a discourse of duality that we argue is inherent in the British Muslim psyche and which is of essential and positive benefit to society as a whole. Dual education is an alternative idea proposed according to the paradigm of dual citizenship (Ameli & Merali, 2004). Dual education is a framework of reimagining a secular education system alongside an Islamic schooling structure which is a reflection of minority rights within the majority and public system of education, as articulated through the aspirations and desires of Muslim themselves.

Dual citizenship, whereby the existence of Islamic identity and aspirations facilitate a more profound and cohesive sense of citizenship within a pluralistic society (Ameli & Merali 2004), is particularly pertinent given the foregoing discussions about the role of faith in education. Are Muslim parents' desires for faith-based education examples of narrow-minded and potentially dangerous division, or do they provide an avenue for the better development of rounded citizens? Does the need or expectation for the recognition of Islam within the educational sphere mean solely the establishment of more Muslim schools? This research argues for a more subtle appraisal of opportunities based upon a very nuanced understanding of education at a systemic level from both parents and students in what both articulate to be a hostile secular environment as opposed to a secular environment and education system that can form part of the duality needed to fulfil Muslim aspiration, human rights obligations and grounded citizenship for all.

The generally low-profile representation of all faith-based schools, including Muslim schooling in educational enquiry can be seen to be an outcome of what Gallagher (1997) has referred to as 'secular marginalisation' in contemporary intellectual culture i.e. especially in the academic and media world, where a secular culture reigns with the result that religion is subtly ignored as unimportant. Major studies of globalisation and education, policy struggle in education, school effectiveness investigations and schools' leadership analysis take place as if the existence of faith-based schooling systems was peripheral to the central questions being raised. Research into the aspirations of the Muslim community indicate that this sits ill with their expectations of education. Muslim parents, Muslim schools of the future and their school leaders and teachers have to devise ways, in changing conditions, of remaining faithful to the principle of St Thomas More: That they should be 'the king's good servant, but God's first'.

Just as many Church of England schools see it as their mission to educate the local community irrespective of the faith of the students, so we can look f orward to the time when this problem can be addressed by the existence of sufficient state-funded Muslim schools to have a surplus of places so that they can admit non-Muslim students to be educated alongside Muslims. Although a provision for the inclusion of non-Muslim pupils exist in the admissions criteria of some Muslim schools, the demand from Muslims for places makes this a practical impossibility.

Muslims would not be alone amongst religious educators in claiming that by producing young people who are fully affirmed and at ease in their religious and cultural identity, they are producing integrated individuals who can take their place in society from a position of personal strength and confidence. State-funded Muslim schools therefore might be seen as a significant contribution to the development of just such a pluralist society.

The existence of denominational schools within the British system may be regarded as an accident of history occasioned by the role that the churches played in the early decades of mass education and the existence of hundreds of community schools run in church-owned premises. This provision has been solidly entrenched by the emphasis placed by the Roman Catholic Church on confessional schools to affirm identity and inculcate Catholic Christianity in the lives of children from that community.

Muslim schools, both primary and secondary, have been well placed in the public league tables of academic and test results, which are, in contemporary society, an important source of the making or breaking of a school's reputation and public image (Morris, A.B. 1998a). In many areas Muslim schools are in-fact over-subscribed by parents attracted by the Muslim school's reputation for academic success, good discipline and for taking spiritual and moral education seriously. Parents, staff and the community place a high level of expectation on students in Muslim schools, and the students, thus affirmed generally, raise their attainment levels. By receiving government funding the benefits of Muslim schools in this respect are shared with a wider student body, particularly with those whose families could not afford to pay school fees. Can the state embrace the opportunity of using a religious ethos and an Islamic perspective as part of its strategy to raise the educational standards of children from disadvantaged minority communities?

Unfortunately the current average attainment levels in these communities, especially of boys of Pakistani heritage, fall well below the average. (See Hewer, C., 2001, 'Schools for Muslims', *Oxford Review of Education*, Vol. 27, no. 4). What is interesting nowadays is the importance that religion plays in terms of personal identity (Modood *et al.* 1997), and how faith-based schools are being chosen by parents who see them as places providing compatibility between the religious values promoted in the home and those practised in schools. Diversity as espoused through government rhetoric is felt to be important to embrace, yet communities fear loss of cultural identity through policies of assimilation and integration (Parekh, 2000). Schools are seen as the place where cultural and religious values come into play and identity may be undermined (Miller, 2001; Sarwar, 1994). What unites rather than divides faith-based schools and their communities is that they all share a desire to perpetuate faith and this is often associated with cultural and linguistic heritage (Parker-Jenkins, Hartas and Irving, 2005).

A charge that is only laid against faith schooling is that it does not prepare students for life in wider society after school years. Indeed some make the claim it promotes a fragmentation of society and reinforces 'separate identity'. All religious schools are open to this charge, but perhaps Muslim schools are particularly targeted given the irrational fear of Islam (Islamophobia) within wider Western society. This is an issue that many Muslim schools take seriously and seek to address by devising collaborative partnerships, exchanges and trips to introduce students to the richness of British and European heritage.

Arthur (1995) notes that as recently as March 1989 the Association of Metropolitan Authorities passed a resolution which considered voluntary-aided schools as "damaging" to the interests of education in some localities. Muslim schools have been subjected to ideological critique from some sections of the left and to call for their abolition on the grounds of social divisiveness, covert selection and a general undermining of the reputation and effectiveness of the state system of schooling. HM Chief Inspector of Schools, David Bell reiterated the negativity levelled at faith schools by suggesting they had problems inculcating a sense of citizenship amongst their pupils. This negativity, variously expressed, flies in the face of preferences amongst the Muslims community in education and is a serious issue that policy makers need to address in conjunction with the Muslim community and not in opposition to either their aspirations or their rights.

BACKGROUND:
STUDIES ON FAITH SCHOOLS

The British government White Paper (2001) *Schools Achieving Success* encourages collaborative work with faith schools, and yet, especially in the wake of recent terrorist attacks it is implied that such schools may encourage "fundamentalism". Many commentators on contemporary religion, e.g. (Armstrong, 2000 in Scott-Baumann, 2003), see no evidence for this in the desire of Muslims to educate their children, yet suspicion of Muslims is prevalent and the separateness of communities is used as evidence (Scott-Baumann, 2003). In the past era we were united to make arbitrary choices. In the education system now, the pressing dilemma should not be a choice of only secular standards of learning but how to take action towards inter-cultural tolerance (Scott-Baumann, 2003).

Durkheim, in his classic study *The Elementary Form of the Religious Life* (1971), made an attempt from the standpoint of religious schooling to understand the nature of the sacred and of its relation to the profane in human societies. He concluded in a powerful and evocative passage:

> We have established the fact that the fundamental categories of thought... are of religious origin... nearly all of the great social institutions have been born into religion...if religion has given birth to all that is essential in society, it is because the idea of society is the soul of religion.
>
> (Durkheim, E., 1971)

Given Durkheim's conviction that 'the idea of society is the soul of religion', it is not surprising that he was opposed to forms of radical individualism and there can be little doubt about what his response to Mrs Thatcher's assertion that 'there is no such thing as society' would have been (Thatcher, M., 1993). For Durkheim, religion constituted not only what society was but crucially also what it could be in a perfected and ideal form. While the concept of "utopia" is not explicitly used in *The Elementary Forms of the Religious Life*, it is clear that Durkheim saw religion as contributing to the formation of an ideal world.

Scott-Baumann's experience over the last five years has shown her that Muslim faith schools can, with guidance, train teachers and can work well as a means of stabilising a multifaith, multiethnic community. Definition of differences is vital, but can only be achieved from a position of relative safety and this may be perceived as missing in the non-Muslim UK community just as much as in the Muslim one. Islamophobic tendencies within the non-Muslim community are balanced by phobic tendencies within the Muslim communities towards secular lifestyles. Given the levels of Islamophobia, awareness of issues will help co-existence. The insistence upon visible homogeneity is clear in both cultures, and a paradigm shift is necessary so that both groups can enjoy their many similarities with each other and respect their differences. If consumerism has come to play the part of religion having become, as Miles puts it 'arguably the religion of *the* twentieth century' (1998:1), the government's stress on parental involvement and choice gives predominance to "the market" and emphasises individual rights over the rights of the community as a whole. For nearly two centuries it has been possible for religious bodies not only to establish schools but also to seek funding for them. Official recognition and public funding arrangements were codified in the 1944 Education Act, especially in the definition of a category of Voluntary-Aided Schools.

Schutz (1971) writes about an immigrant, but in reality it describes us all when we attempt to cross any sort of frontier, emotional, intellectual or work-related. Schutz asserts that attempts to enter other people's territory can lead to disorientation and identity crisis.

THE MUSLIM SCHOOL AND SECULARISATION

The development of secularisation in the modern world from the Enlightenment to the present day presents the agencies of sacred culture with a powerful and sharper challenge. Secularisation represents the denial of the validity of the sacred and its associated culture and its replacement by logical, rational, empirical and scientific intellectual cultures in which the notion of the transcendent has no place. Secularisation involves a significant change in the cultural power relations of any society. Berger, in his influential study *The Social Reality of Religion* (1973:113), expresses it in this way: 'By secularisation we mean the process by which sectors of society and culture are removed from the domination of religious institution and symbols.'

While secularisation changes intellectual culture and power relations, it also operates to affect the worldview of many individuals so that religious concepts, religious discourse, and religious sensitivities are simply irrelevant to the everyday business of life. This is what Berger (1973:113) refers to as 'secularisation of consciousness': 'Put simply this means that the modern West has produced an increasing number of individuals who look upon the world and their own lives without the benefit of religious interpretations.'

There is debate about the wider cultural and intellectual significance of the progress of secularisation in modern society. For some, it represents the liberation of humanity from the myths and obscurantism of religious domination; in short, a true form of human enlightenment in which reason comes to occupy the place formerly assigned to God. For others, secularisation represents a crucial loss of the sense of transcendence in human existence and with it the sense of ultimate meaning and purpose for humanity (Grace, 2002). The domination of "reason" from this perspective represents the arrival of a potentially calculative, bloodless and inhumane cultural form.

In human society a school or an educational experience is not ideologically free. Schools are not entirely autonomous, objective, neutral and ideologically free. Schools are not scientific laboratories. They are, crucially, person-forming, citizen-forming and society-forming institutions and as such they always have been and they are likely to always be influenced by external ideologies of various types - religious, secular, humanist, political and atheist.

Secular schools as opposed to religious schools aren't ideologically free zones. While ideological assumptions may not be formally codified into a curriculum subject designated "secular education", they characteristically permeate the ethos and culture of state-provided secular schools and form a crucial part of the hidden curriculum. The hidden curriculum refers to ways in which schools' ethos, organisation and practice educate pupils in addition to the outcomes of the formal taught and visible curriculum (Grace, G., 2002:14). The term "Islamic school" better describes a desire to develop a school along the lines of Qur'anic scriptures, with a strong nurturing of an Islamic ethos, which permeates the school curricula both formal and hidden. Subjects are taught from an Islamic perspective and the 'relation of all created beings and things…is given and immutable' (Hewer 2001).

People (e.g. Dawkins, 2001) who assert a secular approach to education have a range of arguments against faith schools. Regarding the educational issues and human rights, secularists argue that in faith schools there is a tendency to teach "opinion" as "fact". Furthermore, they think faith schools are divisive (the most often used argument) leading to "ghettoisation", which divide the community based on religion. This secularist's postulate encourages prejudice, discrimination and conflict. Segregated schooling leads to segregated housing as parents are tempted to move to catchment areas around schools or churches or mosques. They go on to affirm that first and foremost children are individuals with rights and 'they are not the property of their parents and should not be assumed to have "beliefs" or assigned to religions, before an age at which they are able to decide on them in the light of information and understanding. For the same reasons they should not be required to worship and practise religious rites in schools.'[1] This is an approach more aggressively defined by organisations like the National Secular Society, but which have also found some reflection in the musings of policymakers, including Chief Inspector of Schools, David Bell, whose comments singling out Muslim schools in January 2005 as problematic were applauded by Chair of the Commission for Racial Equality, Trevor Phillips.

A counter-argument against the educational issues posed by secularists is that certain aspects of the curriculum are taught as a fact and not as an opinion. For example, in the teaching of human evolution in GCSE human biology textbooks recommended by the examining board it is stated that the alpha chain, part of the molecule of haemoglobin in human red blood cells, is the same as in chimpanzees, and this fact is explained by stating 'There can be no other explanation for this except that humans are ancestrally related to chimpanzees.'[2] This statement is itself a biased one, positing a theory as a fact, and belies the suggestion that secular education is value free.

The notion that a secular form of liberal education is the only defensible educational experience that can be offered in modern society has been criticised from a philosophical perspective by McLaughlin (1990). For him it is clearly a right of parents in a democratic and pluralist society to shape the early education of their children according to their beliefs, values, principles and ideologies, which they regard as important. It is also clearly a democratic right of parents to commit their children to faith-based schooling of a religious nature. However, McLaughlin is also aware of the rights of children and young people as they mature to come to their own reasoned position on religious and ideological issues and morality.

If Muslim schools instil in children the value of education, why should they be singled out as potentially causing insular children? Do Muslim children who attend Christian schools in Pakistan have any danger of becoming closed to their society? Are Jewish children who attend Jewish schools somehow socially stunted or unable to cope with British society? The answer is usually held and at least more likely to be held, no and no. The Archbishop of Canterbury, Head of the Anglican Church has spoken out in support of faith schools, including those set up by Muslims. The Archbishop believes that ignoring religions, and the important role religion plays for many, will lead to further fragmentation in society.[3] A large number of young Muslims have retained their Muslim identity and faith but have not seen this as an obstacle to contributing and integrating positively into mainstream British society.

Not only have Muslim schools been a focus of controversy in the expansion of faith-based schooling but also Catholic schools have been criticised as

---

[1]

Campaign for Secular Education http://www.c.s.e.freeuk.com

[2]

Natural History Museum Publications, *Man's Place in Evolution*, 1981, Cambridge University Press, Cambridge

[3]

BBC News/Education; 2/6/02; 6/30/03; 9/11/03

authoritarian and socially divisive. 'If misrepresentations of catholic schooling can exist in political and public debate, it suggests that misrepresentation of the contemporary schooling systems of other faith schools can also exist.' (Grace, 2002b: 8).

Muslim communities are presently particularly vulnerable to attack both verbally and physically, as a result of the war against terrorism. Muslim schools also see themselves as raising academic attainment in what they feel is a preferred environment because: 'Pupils there do not suffer from being in a minority, nor from elements of racism that may remain in local authority schools. Parents, staff and the community place a high level of expectation on students in Muslim schools, and students thus affirmed generally raise their attendance level.' (Hewer, 2001:524).

Education in Britain promotes an unduly secularist approach to life and develops a more materialistic approach. The feeling that all values are special products and hence merely relative to social situations, make the social outlook increasingly materialistic, heavily influencing children. Secularist attitudes can easily weaken the power to resist evil because they underestimate the importance of the interiority of human life and depend too much on externality. But before we can resist evil we must discern what is evil. This is an internal act, which the secularist philosophy all too often ignores.

The British state education system is failing to meet the needs of Muslim pupils and parents, according to a report calling for special classes in Islamic subjects, more single sex education and prayer rooms in secondary schools. The Muslims on Education policy document, compiled by Muslim academics and educationalists, argues that Britain's largest minority community should have access to more Muslim state schools and that non-Muslim schools should adapt more fully to the community's needs (*The Guardian*, June 8 2004). Education without awareness of God is meaningless to faith-based schools. Mabud (1992) suggests that without the religious dimension 'it is not education at all but indoctrination into a particular worldview' (p. 90). The word indoctrination is apposite since that is precisely what sceptics and non-believers contend is happening within faith-based schools. In countries like the United States and Turkey, for example, which claim to operate only secular curricula, the issue is no less contentious, since it is arguable that no education is ever value free or culture free (Parker-Jenkins, Hartas and Irving, 2005, p. 147).

Muslim schooling can be seen to be compatible with liberal democratic principles not least by providing a particular substantial starting point for the child's eventual development into autonomous agency and democratic citizenship. By virtue of the funding of other faith schools, the government has acknowledged that faith schools are compatible or can be compatible. It is not simply just a case of parity between minorities but fostering those differential rights which can guarantee their equality. This has been part of the process that sees Jewish schools promoted and funded by the state.

According to the 2001 census, there are approximately 1.6 million Muslims in Britain, constituting about 3 percent of the population[4]. Muslims are also

---

[4]

Although according to the census Muslims are 1.6 million (see: http://www.statistics.gov.uk/downloads/theme_compendia/for2004/FocusonReligion.pdf); Ansari suggests 2 million as being more realistic since it is thought that 'a significant number of 'undocumented' and asylum seeking Muslims remain unaccounted for'. (see: H. Ansari, *The Infidel within: Muslims in Britain since 1800*, London, Hurst, 2004, p. 172, fn.12).

the largest minority faith group; 6.3% of full-time[5] students in England and Wales are Muslim i.e. 168,496 students are Muslim out of a total student population of 2,659,923. Of the 11,795,236 people aged between 0–17 in the UK there are 587,687 Muslims (i.e. 4.98% of the total are Muslims). Of the 1,098,864 people aged between 0–17 in Scotland 14,967 (i.e. 1.4%) are Muslim.

The issue of Muslim schools vis-à-vis numbers of Muslim school children can be exemplified through the example of England. According to National Statistics there were 371,000 school-aged (5 to 16 year-old) Muslim children in England in 2001 and four Muslim state-maintained schools in 2003, catering for around 1,000 children. There were 64,000 school-aged Sikh children and two Sikh state-maintained schools, catering for 600 children. There were 33,000 Jewish school-aged children in England compared with 13,000 places in state-maintained Jewish schools. The actual figure given for state-maintained Jewish schools varies. In response to a question posed by Hendon MP, Andrew Dismore in the House of Commons, erstwhile Education Secretary, Estelle Morris MP gave the following breakdown[6]:

	Total number of Jewish schools	Number of maintained Jewish schools
1997	70	26
1998	72	27
1999	74	28
2000	78	31
2001	78	32

However, in the 2003/2004 Ofsted report[7] by HM Chief Inspector of Schools David Bell the figure of 51 Jewish schools catering for around 9,500 pupils was given. The overall number of Muslim schools is estimated to be 111, catering for about 14,000 students[8].

Set in the context of young people's statistics according to the 2001 census, there were 587,687 Muslims between ages 0–17 (4.98% of All People 0–17) and 50,177 Jews between ages 0–17 (0.43% of All People 0–17) in England and Wales. There seems to be a serious disparity between state funding for Muslim schools and acknowledgement by state funding for Jewish schools.

5

* full-time denotes both economically active and inactive students.

6

http://www.parliament.the-stationery-office.co.uk/pa/cm200001/cmhansrd/vo010327/text/10327w07.htm

7

http://www.ofsted.gov.uk/publications/annualreport0304/1.922.htm

8

Ibid.

During the 1960s and 1970s the academic attainment levels of Muslim children were low and their general progress was unsatisfactory. The gap between Muslim pupils and the rest persisted through the 1980s and the 1990s. Moreover, the overall gap in educational achievements had widened between the Indians and Whites, on the one hand, and Pakistani, Bangladeshi and Afro-Caribbean students on the other. In Bradford in 1996, 13% of Pakistani and 15% of Bangladeshi males, compared with 37% of Indians and 25% of Whites, achieved five or more GCSE passes at grade A-C (figures for both Pakistani Bangladeshi females were 19% compared with 44% and 33% for Indian and White females respectively). In Waltham Forest in 1994, however, more Pakistanis obtained O-level passes than Whites (33.5% as opposed to 29.8%) and in 1995 even Bangladeshis in the borough outperformed White pupils (30.6% as opposed 30.0%) (Runnymede, 1997, Anwar, 1996).

Studies carried out during the 1980s and 1990s now suggest that Muslim pupils' experience within school had more impact on their academic performance than previously thought. Given the persistence of inequalities in education along ethnic lines, the immigrant/stranger theory of under-achievement was gradually diverted of its explanatory power. (Smith and Tomlinson, 1989.) According to Tomlinson, evidence had accumulated that normal school processes can have the effect of disadvantaging pupils from particular ethnic groups (Tomlinson, 1987).

Research indicated that many ethnic minority pupils have been subjected to systemic discrimination within schools. Familiar patterns of discrimination and negative stereotyping by teachers were evident in the selection and allocation of courses. In addition to Muslim children's personal development the schools' social environment also caused concern to many Muslims, especially the harassment experienced by Muslim pupils. The Commission for Racial Equality's investigation into racial harassment, *Learning in Terror: Survey of Racial Harassment in Schools and Colleges* (1988), gave ample evidence of the prevalence of racial abuse and violence in schools and the distress and torment it caused. It revealed too how indifferent and insensitive teachers were to the plight of their pupils, and indeed that some teachers expressed racist opinions to their white colleagues and made humiliating remarks and jokes not only to pupils in the classroom but also to their minority colleagues in the staff room (Donald and Rattanzi, 1989).

SCHOOL CURRICULUM

An HM inspection (HMI) survey of 1972 found that the subject content of history, geography and religious education was becoming rapidly "out of touch" with a changing world, and noted that very little modification of the curriculum has taken place and there is little evidence that subject departments in general have considered the curriculum critically in the light of the presence of immigrant pupils in their classes (Taylor and Hegarty,1985). Moreover, research suggested that the historical experience of Muslims was being ignored and devalued and what little was offered about Islam and the

---

9

Ibid, p. 103, for illustrative material see J. Eggleston, J. Dunn, M. Anjali and C. Wright, *Education For Some,* Stroke on Trent, 1986. For more recent research on teachers perceptions of Muslim pupils see Basit, *Eastern Values, Western Milieu,* p. 144-64.

history of Muslim societies was presented from a secular framework and the perspectives of European conquerors. The world of the Muslim minorities in Britain – their cultures, language and religion – was in effect marginalised and deprecated (Ansari, 2004). More generally textbooks continued to present a broadly ethnocentric view of Islam.

The 1985 Swann Report revealed how Greeks and Turks had been portrayed in the curriculum with the Greeks viewed as 'the great civilisers of the world' and at the heart of Western tradition and the Turks as 'uncivilised' and cruel 'barbarians' followers of a strange 'foreign' faith (Swann, 1985:689).

There is no mention of a single Muslim scientist or a mathematician in the National Curriculum. It is not until Higher Education at university in the teaching of mathematics that the contribution of Muslim scholars is mentioned much to the surprise of non-Muslims as was reported by one subject in the survey. Muslims were worried that textbooks and courses were undermining their children's identity 'creating doubts in the minds of students about the fundamental tenets and assumptions of Islam', and also affirming white children in the prejudices they picked up from the media, comics and the cinema (Ashraf and Hussain, 1979).

This ethnocentric curriculum had a negative effect on Muslim pupils' academic performance, not least by reinforcing feelings of being outsiders and different. The Education Reform Act 1988, with its establishment of the National Curriculum allowed room for the inclusion of Muslim perspectives in the teachings of history. It was possible to maintain a Eurocentric bias in subject content and some commentators remarked that National Curriculum documents to date, with very few exceptions, are drawn up in an assimilationist spirit (Grinter, 1990:26).

EDUCATION REFORM ACT 1988

"… all pupils in attendance at a maintained school shall on each school day take part in an act of collective worship"[10]

By the 1990s, however, some changes were discernible such as options in Urdu, Persian and Arabic, recognising their relevance to Muslim pupils. Research in 1972 had revealed that few schools made provision for even a superficial study of religions other than Christianity in their religious education (RE) curriculum. Withdrawal from school assemblies and RE lessons was legally allowed but, given the ethos of many schools, few took advantage of this (Townsend and Brittan, 1972).

In light of this "neglect", many Muslim parents were worried about the drift away from parental authority, which they attributed to the marginalisation of religious education coupled with a lack of inculcation of discipline in state schools.

The government abandoned the policy of assimilation and moved towards a multiculturalist approach, echoed in the famous words of Roy Jenkins, Home Secretary in 1966: 'equal opportunity accompanied by cultural diversity in an atmosphere of mutual tolerance'. (Patterson, 1969).

[10]

Education Reform Act 1988 part 1, section 6

SINGLE-SEX SCHOOLING

Single sex education continues to be an aspiration for some Muslim parents, who see the phasing out of such schools as contrary to their interests (Modood *et al.,* 1997). The mixing of sexes at school, especially at the secondary level, was seen as a major threat to the social fabric and stability of Muslim communities. This brought them into conflict with the authorities whose attitude was that coeducation promoted the goal of gender equality and benefited all pupils, especially girls. In the absence of schools promoting an Islamic faith, Muslim parents have chosen alternative faith-based schools, such as those run on Anglican or Catholic lines, which are seen to be supportive of both moral education and single-sex schooling.

MUSLIM EDUCATION IN BRITAIN: MID-1980S TO 2001

With the coming of the Conservatives in 1979 the multicultural agenda began to be rolled back. The New Right became ideologically dominant, and its thinking found its way increasingly into government policies. Its leaders on the ideas of multicultural and antiracist education mounted a major assault on the ideological front (Gordon and Klug, 1986; S. Randall, 1998). Tamney proposed that the Conservative government instituted programs to achieve Conservative goals, which however failed to advance Conservative policies. This was because the expectations for religious education were inconsistent with other educational values and also because of the contemporary religious institutions (Tamney, 1992b).

In a modern society schools are valued as a means of achieving material success, and the primary purpose of the curriculum is the production of a skilled pool of potential workers. Because religion is not relevant to either goal, Tamney argues that students or those in charge of the curriculum will not take it seriously (Tamney,1994). Thatcher singled out 'The truths of the Judaic-Christian tradition' as the source of the moral impulse that alone can lead to peace (Thatcher, 1988). The reform of religious education was part of a Conservative programme to strengthen traditional Toryism: Victorian morality and patriotism (Marquand, 1988).

In 1990 the government introduced the theme of citizenship, which was to be infused into all school subjects. Since what it means to be a citizen involves ethical obligations, this new requirement furthers the differentiation of ethics and religion, thereby lessening the social importance of RE classes. Religious education lacks the resources that are necessary for success. Collectively, RE teachers have been the least qualified in comparison with teachers responsible for other subjects in the National Curriculum; 56 per cent of RE teachers had no qualifications at all in the subject according to the Association of Christian Teachers (Grace, 2002). A shortage of qualified RE teachers remains a critical problem (Lodge, 1991).

THE STRUGGLE FOR VOLUNTARY-AIDED MUSLIM SCHOOLS

Campaigns to establish voluntary-aided Muslim schools began in the 1970s and became more vociferous from the 1980s. 80 per cent of Muslim parents were in favour of Muslim schools according to the Muslim Educational Trust. The number of independent Muslim schools expanded from 45 in 1996 to 53 in 1997 and 77 in 2002 according to the Association of Muslim Schools.

Presently there are 111 independent Muslim schools which include two each in Scotland and Wales. All are Sunni with the exception of one Shia school, namely Al Sadiq and Al Zahra school which reflects the fact that only 10 per cent of the Muslim communities in Britain are Shia (Weller *et al.*, 2001).

Campaigners for Muslim schools rejected the assertion that they would be divisive; they would follow the National Curriculum, but by developing an Islamic ethos they would give Muslim children a positive sense of their own identity, so important for integration within a truly multicultural society (see Akhtar, 1992). In this way Muslims contested the understanding of how 'integration' as presented by the British establishment, might occur. Indeed, they received support from representatives of groups who already enjoyed religious schools, such as David Konstant, the Roman Catholic Bishop of Leeds. For him, 'having our own school within the state system helped us to move out of our initial isolation so as to become more confident and self-assured. The effect of separate schools [had] been integration and not divisiveness.' (Konstant quoted in *Times Educational Supplement*, 1991). Strangely, many of the staunchest opponents of Muslim schools have been those who supported the idea of multicultural education, albeit in a secular framework, rather than John Patten's assimilationist view, which contended that there could be no 'room for separation and segregation'. (*The Times*, 1989).

The Observer in May 2002 carried an article reporting that under the new rules that have been brought in to 'stamp out segregation', which is seen as one of the main contributing factors in the disturbances in 2001 in the north of England, all-white schools in inner cities will be forced to take ethnic minority pupils. This had the aim of preventing "ghetto" lifestyles where children never mix with other cultures breeding 'mutual hatred and suspicion'. However, others, notably Eric Seward, regional director for the Commission for Racial Equality (CRE) and author of the CRE report *A Place For Us All* said that it was economic factors rather than cultural factors that had contributed to the segregation (British Muslims Monthly Survey, May 2002). Segregated schooling was disproportionately scapegoated by the government when other factors such as disproportionate funding strategies that marginalised minority ethnic communities and the perpetuation of misconceptions regarding such funding were highlighted by both local activists and researchers into the disturbances (Ahmed *et al.*, 2001). The spectre of increased segregation through faith schools was raised without there being evidence to back the claim. Rioters were the products of main-stream schooling, and as one headteacher of a highly successful Muslim school claimed,[11] faith schools could be the solution to the crisis that caused some young men of minority communities to erupt into violence.

At the start of the new millennium therefore many of the issues with which British Muslims had been grappling in the 1970s and 1980s still caused concern. Some Muslim parents remained determined to send their daughters to single-sex schools despite the steep decline in its time of provision. As in the 1970s, in 2001 Khalil Hussain, 12 year-old Ayesha's father was to be found resisting on religious grounds pressure from the authorities to send her to a local mixed school in Manchester even though he risked a fine or a jail sentence.

---

[11]

Abdullah Trevathan speaking on 'Pros and cons of faith schools' Hard Talk, BBC, 6 February 2002, http://news.bbc.co.uk/1/hi/education/1804427.stm

Eventually grant-maintained status was given to Al-Furqan school Bradford and Islamia School Brent in London in early 1998 after much indecision by the government. Faversham College for girls in Bradford and Al-Hijrah school in Birmingham were awarded the same status in the autumn of 2001 (British Muslims Monthly Survey, September 2001). However, in the light of Lord Ouseley's report on the Bradford disturbances of 2001, which suggested that segregation in schools was a major cause of racial tension, opposition to faith schools resurfaced. *(British Muslims Monthly Survey,* February 2002). The arguments were not new, with opponents still objecting to Muslim schools as divisive and inimical to 'integration'. Bill Morris, the black general secretary of the transport and general workers union and a powerful figure in the British labour movement, described plans to increase faith schools as a 'time bomb' (*The Daily Telegraph, 2001*). Phil Willis, the Liberal Democrat education spokesman also thought there was 'a real danger here of education apartheid.'

Towards the end of the decade the political climate became more supportive, partly because the British public now took a more favourable view of the quality of the education provided by faith schools generally and partly because of the Labour government's thinking on ways of improving all-round educational provision. But, after the September 2001 terrorist attacks in America and the demonstrable rise in popular hostility towards Muslims in Britain, the enthusiasm for faith schools declined once again.

PUBLIC ATTITUDES TOWARD EUROPEAN MUSLIMS' RELIGIOUS PRACTICES AFTER SEPTEMBER 11

Popular fear of Muslims has intensified in the aftermath of the September 11 attacks. Determining the extent of opposition to state accommodation of Muslim religious practices and isolating the causes of such hostility have thus become all the more critical to West European politics. The issue at the fore-front of debate in Britain is state aid to separate Islamic schools (Dwyer and Meyer, 1995). For decades, the state has financed thousands of Anglican and Catholic schools and dozens of Jewish ones. Muslims assert that the state, which currently funds only a handful of Islamic schools, should provide aid to their institutions under the same conditions. Fetzer and Soper (2003) carried out a survey in Britain about whether the government should approve funding for more Islamic schools, limit its approval or cancel its approval: 32 per cent of its respondents supported an extensive policy; 48 per cent supported the policy status quo, which indicated that issues surrounding Muslims 'religious rights are both unsettled and contentious'; 20 per cent wanted the restriction of such approval. Fetzer and Soper (2003) concluded that with the obvious exceptions of Muslims, religious minorities did not usually support the expansion of Islam in schools, and conversely their results did not confirm their hypothesis that the religious majority is signifi-cantly more hostile to such expansion. They also concluded nowhere were secularists more likely than the majority religious group to oppose state accommodation of Muslims' religious practices. The respondents were far more tolerant toward Islam than reports in the popular press might suggest.

STUDIES ON CURRENT INEQUITIES IN CONTEMPORARY SCHOOLS.

It is important to recognise that *every* ethnic group is capable of the highest achievement (Gillborn and Mirza, 2000). One should guard against stereo-typing because of statistics.

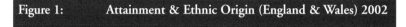

Figure 1:   **Attainment & Ethnic Origin (England & Wales) 2002**

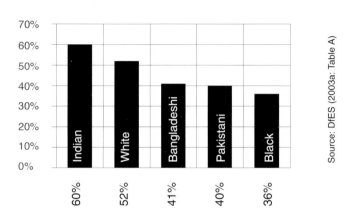

Source: DfES (2003a: Table A)

Nationally, discussion of "under-achievement" is usually focused on three principal minority ethnic groups: Black (African Caribbean), Bangladeshi and Pakistani youth and children. Although the rates are different every year and vary from one region to another, overall it is clear that children and youth that are part of these groups tend to achieve less well, on average, than their white peers of the same gender and background of social-standing. This is a well-established pattern at the national level and has been found from numerous surveys. In 2002, 52% of White 16 year-olds attained five or more higher grade (A*-C) passes in their GCSEs. In comparison, this level was attained by 36% of Black youth, 40% of Pakistanis and 41% of Bangladeshis.

In late 2000, Ofsted published a new review of evidence on the influence of race, class and gender on educational attainment (Gillborn and Mirza, 2000). Commissioned as part of Ofsted's response to the Stephen Lawrence Inquiry (Macpherson, 1999) and building on an earlier review of "race" research (Gilborn, D. and Gipps, C. 1996 *Recent Research on the Achievements of Ethnic Minority Pupils.* Report for the Office of Standards in Education, London: HMSO), the report drew considerable publicity with its claim that sustainable inequities of attainment between minority groups were not only persisting but, in some cases, actually growing:

> *Indian pupils have made the greatest gains in the last decade: enough to overtake their White peers as a group. Bangladeshi pupils have improved significantly but the gap between themselves and White youngsters is much the same...*

> *African-Caribbean and Pakistani pupils have drawn least benefit from the rising levels of attainment:*

The gap between them and their White peers is bigger now than a decade ago (Gillborn and Mirza, 2000).

It should be noted, however, that gender and social class are both factors which are strongly associated with differences in average attainment and it is important to remember that these are often absent from official statistics.

Qualitative Studies

Studies of schools suggest that racial harassment is a regular (for some a daily) occurrence. Calling names across classrooms, tripping students in the corridor, drawing graffiti on the wall: all of these are forms of racist abuse that have been seen to go unpunished in some schools. Following the Stephen Lawrence Inquiry, the Home Office issued a new code of practice on reporting racist incidents. The document recommended the following definition:

> A racist incident is any incident which is perceived to be racist by the victim or any other person … The purpose of this definition is not to prejudge whether a perpetrator's motive was racist or not: that may have to be proved … rather [it is] to ensure that investigations take account of the possibility of a racist dimension to the incident and that statistics of such incidents are collected on a uniform basis.
>
> (Home Office Code of Practice on Reporting and Recording Racist Incidents)

Too often, racist incidents (especially racist name calling) have been denied significance by White people who have failed to understand the meaning of such assaults. Almost 20 years ago the Swann Report (1985) complained of this approach and it is still in evidence: the following quotation, for example, is taken from a study of white teachers' views (Kemp and Gillborn, 2000), questioned up to a year after the publication of the Stephen Lawrence report:

> I haven't seen any instance of what I would call a serious racist incident. I've heard silly name-calling. I suppose it's got to be taken seriously, but within reason: kids do call each other names, to start panicking and saying 'it's terrible, it's being racist' is just not the case. (White primary school teacher).

To simply deny the possibility that the student has a genuine grievance, however, is not only disrespectful, but also refuses any possibility of engagement and, effectively, rejects the case for anti-racism (Gillborn, 2004). The thrust of many contemporary critiques (and increasingly a view enshrined in equity legislation in Britain) is that racism can actually be much more subtle and even unintended. This is the position underlying the Stephen Lawrence Inquiry report's definition of "institutional racism":

> The collective failure of an organisation to provide an appropriate and professional service to people because of their colour, culture, or ethnic origin. It can be seen or detected in processes, attitudes and behaviour which amount to discrimination through unwitting prejudice, ignorance, thoughtlessness and racist stereotyping which disadvantage minority ethnic people (Macpherson, 1999: 28).

This definition is highly relevant to education because research has increasingly revealed numerous ways in which teachers' assumptions (e.g. about behavior, "ability" and motivation) can operate to the disadvantage of particular minority ethnic groups. Research, in both the USA and UK (and for at least two decades), has shown consistently that when teachers are asked to judge the relative ability, motivation and behaviour of their students, it is likely that Black students will be systematically disadvantaged. Black students are typically *under*-represented in high status teaching groups (Hallam, 2002; Hallam and Toutounji, 1996; Oakes, 1990; Sukhnandan and Lee, 1998).

For South-Asian students, there is evidence that language needs are frequently misinterpreted, leading to stereotyping and the denial of learning opportunities. There is often a failure to distinguish between *language* needs and *learning* difficulties. This can lead to students with English as an Additional Language (EAL) being defined as having Special Educational Needs (SEN) and then being passed over for subsequent opportunities because of issues related to teacher expectations, curriculum coverage and examination attainment (Cline and Shamsi, 2000; Gillborn and Youdell, 2000; Hallam and Toutounji, 1996; Troyna and Siraj-Blatchford, 1993). In the mid-1990s new data, based on Ofsted inspections, suggested that nationally Black Caribbean children were excluded from secondary schools at almost *six times* the rate for white students (Gillborn and Gipps, 1996: 53). More recently, Ofsted reported that 'many Black pupils who find themselves subject to disciplinary procedures perceive themselves to have been unfairly treated': inspectors noted that 'the lengths of fixed-period exclusions [suspensions] varied considerably in some schools between Black and White pupils for what were described as the same or similar incidents' (Ofsted, 2001: 23). Once again, these official reports lend substance to several qualitative research studies that have suggested that Black students receive systematically harsher treatment, not through any conscious conspiracy to discriminate, but through the actions of teachers who tend to perceive a greater threat in their Black students (Blair, 2001; Parekh *et al.*, 2000; Sewell, 1998; Wright *et al.*, 2000).

The best available evidence, therefore, demonstrates, first, that considerable inequities in attainment and opportunity continue to scar the English educational system. Second, the school system and education policy appear to be actively implicated in the process which sustain, and in some cases extend, race inequity: including differences in attainment at the end of compulsory schooling, growing inequities as students move through the system, and the continued over-exclusion of Black children. Some of the processes can appear subtle, for example, teachers' differential expectations and the cumulative effects of internal selection within schools. In Britain multiculturalism has often been defined negatively in contrast to a more radical critique offered by theorists and activists under the heading of "anti-racism".

Such critiques portray multiculturalism as a liberal facade that deflects deeper criticism by attending to superficial matters of "celebrating diversity" and making limited token (often patronising) curricular changes. On its publication, in February 1999, the Stephen Lawrence Inquiry Report (Macpherson, 1999) sent shock waves through Britain with its meticulous account of the bungled police investigation and its conclusion that:

> racism, institutional or otherwise, is not the prerogative of the Police Service. It is clear that other agencies including for example those dealing with housing and education also suffer from the disease (Macpherson, 1999: 33).

Remarkably, for a report that began with a racist murder (surely the most crude and vicious form of racism), the Lawrence Inquiry insisted on a broad reworking of the term "institutional racism" (noted above), that explicitly included unintended and thoughtless acts that have the *effect* of discriminating regardless of their intent. As Stokely Carmichael and Charles V. Hamilton observed more than 30 years ago, institutional racism: is less overt, far more subtle, less identifiable in terms of *specific* individuals committing the acts. But it is no less destructive of human life. [It] originates in the operation of established and respected forces in the society, and thus receives far less public condemnation … (Carmichael and Hamilton, 1967 original emphasis, reprinted in Cashmore and Jennings, 2001: 112).

Legislative changes have made public authorities (including all state-maintained schools) legally answerable for race inequity and established a series of requirements that provide a powerful framework for placing antiracism on the agenda of all schools and local education authorities.

Public figures and the good intentions of new legislation have yet to make any meaningful and consistent impact on the brutal realities of racist inequity experienced by many students. The central tenets of education policy continue to be driven by a top-down reformist agenda that prioritises crude and regressive notions of "standards" above any serious attempt to reduce inequity and improve social inclusion. The drive to produce "results" that will look good in the formal school performance tables continues to distort school curricula; selection within schools continues to spread (to more parts of the curriculum and throughout the entire compulsory age range); inequities in attainment remain significant, in some cases they are worse than a decade ago; and Black children remain significantly more likely to be excluded from mainstream schooling altogether.

REASSERTING COMMON HERITAGE: LESSONS FROM AMERICA

 I had not realised that the scientific advances which I learnt at school were brought by the Moors into Europe, had in fact originated in a great cultural flourishing in Central Asia. The great medic, Avicenna, and the inventor of Algebra and other mathematical advances, both hailed from Uzbekistan, not to mention the astronomy of the Emperor Ulughbek, the elegant remains of whose observatory are for me the most arresting of all the wonders of Samarkand. This same golden period saw great advances in architecture, which spread, throughout the Islamic world. Sadly, centuries of earthquake and the almost equally devastating heavy-handed restoration of the Soviet period, disastrously still continued by UNESCO, have left little of the original.

Talk by Craig Murray, former British Ambassador to Uzbekistan to the Royal Institute for International Affairs, Chatham House, London, 8 November 2004.

Stereotypes and misrepresentations of Islam have been deeply ingrained in American culture. The cultural and social conditions for learning about Islam and Muslims in American schools slowly began to change in the 1970s. This pattern is most conspicuous in the instructional materials that teachers and students read. To the extent that young Americans are exposed to interpretations of Islam and Muslim history independent of the mass media, they get them from the commercial textbooks that schools adopt, as well as from ancillary print and visual materials selected by teachers. In the 1970s, media representations of Islam and Muslims were growing steadily more negative and cliché-ridden, owing to the fourth Arab-Israeli war, the oil embargo and the Iranian revolution. Ironically, it was in this same decade that educators built a persuasive case for improving global history, foreign language training and knowledge of world affairs. After the Second World War, majority sentiment among educators favoured the idea that ignoring religion in schools was a good way to avoid conflict. Consequently, religions were nearly written out of many social studies programs altogether. This trend contrasted sharply with the situation in post-war Britain, where religious education was the one subject required by parliamentary statute in all state-maintained schools.

Also in 1988, seventeen religious and educational organisations, including the Islamic Society of North America, approved guidelines that articulate the distinctions between "teaching religion" and "teaching about religion" (Haynes and Thomas 1994, 6:1, 10:1). In brief, these criteria require an academic, not devotional, approach to religious study, the goal being student understanding of various belief systems and their history.

ISLAM IN WORLD HISTORY TEXTBOOKS

The time an average student spends studying about Islam and Muslim history in American schools amounts to just a few weeks in twelve years of schooling. This instruction usually takes place in the context of world history or world culture/geography surveys between grades six and twelve (ages 11-18). Textbooks do not stimulate social studies educators to rethink conceptions of world history or to integrate the narrative along more global lines. Texts have paid little attention to major processes of change that cannot be confined within the experience of one "culture group" or another. Such a unitary approach, what André Gunder-Frank (1992) has called "humanocentric history," might effectively satisfy the inclusionary demands of multiculturalists and at the same time be more relevant to the interactive, deterritorialised, globalising world in which we live.

Susan L. Douglass & Ross E. Dunn (2001) reviewed text books which reveals that Islam is generally not interpreted as its adherents understand it but as the editors believe will be acceptable to textbook adoption committees. Moreover, certain fundamental facts are ignored, while other details are selectively emphasised.

Intentionally or otherwise, Judaism, Christianity and Islam each appear as autonomous cultural packages. Moreover, subtle and not so subtle statements denigrate or "explain away" Islam in clear violation of the 1988 guidelines.

Treating each religion as a cultural entity situated within a bounded period of the past leads easily to its being perceived as homogeneous ("all Muslims do this, all Christians do that"), essentialised ("If you are a Muslim, here is how you will think and act") and made ahistorical ("Muslims think and behave this way because they have done so for fourteen hundred years").

Textbooks often use the term "new" to introduce the origins story of monotheistic belief systems. Five of the eleven books used in the USA study describe Islam as a "new" religion. In the other five books the implication is the same, since none of the texts make clear Muslims' belief that Islam is religion per se or that it is the faith of Adam and all the subsequent prophets, despite the clarity of Islamic doctrine on this point. In fact, Adam and Eve are virtually excluded from all world history texts, even as cultural referents. This primordial pair is presumably of little use when the aim is to dwell mainly on the dissimilarities among Judaism, Christianity and Islam. The origin of Islam, rather, is described not as Muslims are likely to do it but in relation to historical matrices that intersect in the seventh century.

It is difficult to escape the conclusion that the world history textbooks deliberately downplay or exclude connections between Islam and Abraham in order to maintain neat partitions among the symbols, beliefs and major figures of the three monotheistic faiths. Muslim and other scholarly reviewers of textbooks have repeatedly argued that the Abrahamic tradition must be a part of the basic account of Islam's origins and practice. Many publishers continue to disregard the advice, though some new editions indicate that they are beginning to change. Indeed, the omission is made in clear violation of the 1988 guidelines for teaching about religion. Editors may have concluded that the textbook adoption market in politically and religiously conservative states will not bear ambiguity about Abraham's strict identification with the Old Testament and the Judaeo-Christian tradition. The second matrix for explaining the origins of Islam is the biography of Muhammad, which all the texts recount. None of these narratives expressly describe Qur'anic teachings on the beginnings of Islam. Explicitly or subtly, all the texts define Muhammad as the founder of Islam, just as Abraham, Jesus and the Buddha are cited as the founders of their respective religions. Four of the books apply the terms "founded" or "founder" to characterise Muhammad's career (Banks *et al.* 1997, 271; Bednarz *et al.*, 1997, 78; Hanes 1997, 47; Wallbank *et al.* 1987, 34, 137). None of them gives a definition of the term, though many students are likely to understand it as synonymous with "inventor," one who brings something into existence, rather than one who established something or caused it to be recognised and accepted. None of these books reflects the Muslims' belief that God is the source of revelation.

The distancing term of choice in some of the books is "vision", a word that is not used to describe revelation or contact with God in the discussions of early Judaism or Christianity. One account features multiple repetitions of the term.

> At the age of 40, Muhammad's life was changed overnight by a vision. … In his vision, the angel Gabriel told him that he was a messenger of God. Muhammad had other visions in which Gabriel appeared with messages from Allah (Arabic for God). Who was Allah? Muhammad believed Allah was the same God worshipped by Christians and Jews.
>
> (Krieger et al., 1997, 186)

Islam, presented as separate from the Abrahamic tradition, is shown to have picked up similarities with Judaism and Christianity through alleged imitation or borrowing. Three of the accounts state unequivocally that the earlier traditions were absorbed into the later religion as doctrine. One of the statements is particularly crass, "explaining away" Islam in violation of the guidelines: "In his travels [Muhammad] met many people of different cultures, including Jews and Christians. These contacts were to have a profound influence on the religion that he later developed" (Wallbank *et al.*, 1987, 188).

A broad interpretative thread in all the textbooks is the use of the terms "Islam" and "Islamic." In most of the books the word is applied to all manner of historical phenomena:

"Islamic empire", "Islamic trade routes" "Islamic art and science"and "Islamic men and women" are some examples of usage suggesting that anything that happened in regions where Muslim populations predominated may reasonably be attributed to religion. This practice is of course fairly pervasive in the scholarly literature generally. None of the texts uses the term "Christian" in the same way.

Ever since the 1970s, when multiculturalist ethno-racial critics protested the common schoolbook claim that Europe possessed a monopoly on scientific genius, publishers have included mention of inventions and other achievements as standard fare in chapters on premodern, non-Western cultures. The most commonly cited Muslim achievements are astronomical knowledge, medical advances, algebra, bank cheques and lateen sails, described in many books as *"Arab."*

An exception is the transfer of Greek philosophical and scientific works to the West by way of Muslim scholars and their enlightened patrons. Revised 1999 editions of a few textbooks demonstrate change in this direction. Almost all the textbooks state or at least imply that the Muslim "golden age" exhausted itself by about the eleventh century.

Condition for progress is to raise the level of scholarship upon which textbook accounts are based, including critical use of primary source documents and fundamental understanding that all historical writing, including textbooks, inevitably involves interpretation, judgment, and social reconstruction of the past. Finally, if educators attend carefully to accepted standards for teaching about religion, more authentic and less confusing accounts will result. Textbook authors should write about Islam and all other faiths not to induce belief or disbelief, but to record as accurately as they can both the findings of modern scholarship and the understandings that Muslims have of doctrine, moral behaviour, spiritual aspiration and the origins and establishment of their faith. The U.S. Supreme Court argued that the central reason for teaching about religion is that without it neither the long run of human history nor contemporary global culture will make sense to future generations.

This is a simple and obvious proposition, but putting it to a full test will require abandoning the current habit in American education of essentialising religions, civilisations and ethno-racial groups in the interests of either patriotism or cultural self-esteem. A human-centered and dynamic global history in the schools holds some promise of counteracting and ultimately bringing to an end the caricatures and misrepresentations of Islam that flow from the popular media.

THE STRUGGLE FOR INCLUSIVE CITIZENSHIP

Citizenship is a relatively new National Curriculum subject taught at key stages 3 and 4 from August 2002. Its aim is to enable pupils to develop the knowledge, skills and understanding to become informed, active and responsible members of local, national and global communities. Citizenship can be used as a way of explaining identities and identifying similarities between communities. QCA is developing a web-based project, 'Respect for all', which aims to promote good practice in multicultural and anti-racist education across all curriculum subjects at all key stages. More opportunities should be made for pupils to focus on common elements, concerns and values in human experience and religious traditions whilst appreciating the integrity and distinctiveness of Islam.

A Dual Education System – Islamic and Secular – is a necessity where everybody benefits. A Dual Education System can be defined as: Education of pupils from non-Muslim and Muslim backgrounds with the aim of providing for them both secular and Islamic education that gives equal recognition to Islam and promotes an equal expression to Islam and to secular education. By so doing the universalised aspects of education are promoted through which commonality is reinforced, and where particularism with respect to confessional issues, as well as issues surrounding fair representation of religion across curricula, are not only respected but taught and incorporated, a polycentric model of education is developed that replaces existing ethnocentric models.

The school as an institution seeks to develop mutual respect and consideration of other institutions within the educational community. Its core aim is to provide the child with a caring self-fulfilling educational experience which will enable him/her to become a fulfilled and caring adult. This dual approach would promote the worth and self-development of all individuals within the school community.

Parents have the basic rights in determining the nature of their children's education as set out in the United Nations Declaration on Human Rights and the European Convention on Human Rights. This is something that has been raised vis-à-vis faith education in Northern Ireland with the movement for integrated education. The success and popularity of such projects[12] can be used as an exemplar for an integrated approach to mainstream education across the UK. Faith schools in this context can provide another medium through which pluralistic education that respects and encourages commonality whilst developing confident individuals can take place, and which is essential for the development of a cohesive society of empowered citizens.

A fire inspector at a Muslim school in the borough of Brent in North West London commented that the Muslim school was the first that he has visited which had no evidence of smoking, drug taking or solvent abuse. The fact that they were religious values in that particular school, indicates that there is some social value in having religious values reflected throughout a school, that give it prominence. That school is without social ills that are pervasive in other schools; there must be some benefit in having religious studies which permeated throughout the school.

Professor S. A. Ashraf planned a seminar in 1990 which was called, "Faith as the basis of education in a multi-faith, multi-cultural country." This seminar was organised by The Islamic Academy, Cambridge and the Department of Education, University of Cambridge:

12

Northern Ireland Council for Integrated Education (NICIE)
http://www.nicie.org/aboutus/default.asp?id=27

A suggested common "Faith" framework for the curriculum

The education here conceived presupposes faith and operates within its sphere, rather than faith being treated as something extraneous to education and external to its major objects. It therefore sets forward an approach to education which reflects the presuppositions of faith. Nevertheless, it recognises that there will still be those who will prefer a secular based education. Such should be free to pursue their own goals. For this approach eschews any form of indoctrination or compulsion in religion. A faith which is to be deep and enduring must be chosen and/or held in freedom. As Judaism, Christianity and Islam (and other faiths) believe in one Transcendent Deity, the existence of absolute values derived from God and the reality of the spiritual aspect of human nature, the following curriculum aims are suggested:

1. Beliefs and Values (Cognitive & Affective: Knowledge & Attitudes)

1.1 Awareness of God, the Supreme Being.

1.2 Awareness of the Absolute Values in God's Qualities reflected in the Creation .i.e. Humankind and Nature.

1.3 Awareness that each individual is a unique human being.

1.4 Awareness that we all can manifest within ourselves the values referred to in A2 and that in this lies our humanity.

1.5 Awareness that God has created different racial groups so that we may know each other and live in harmony, respecting the different and differing customs, values, beliefs and languages of the main cultures of the country.

1.6 Awareness that the richness of each community depends on how far it can appreciate and value the achievements of other communities and assimilate them for the benefit of its own existence.

1.7 Awareness of the history and achievements of one's own community and the importance of being a member of that community, and the development in each individual of the ability to evaluate his/her own culture dispassionately.

1.8 Development not only of tolerance and concern for the rights and beliefs of others, but a commitment to practical engagement on their behalf on the basis of the awareness that in the eyes of God all have equal rights and are entitled to justice.

1.9 Development of the capability to see all these cultures in a more global context and to shun all stereotypes be they of race, nation, gender or religion and be aware of the danger of being caught up by ethnocentric feelings which are in conflict with the essential religious values which are also ethical and the source of all the principles enunciated earlier.

2. Intellectual , Emotional and Social (Knowledge and Skills)

2.1 Nurturing and development of the powers of reasoning, reflective and critical thinking, imagining, feeling and communicating among and between persons.

2.2 Learning how to maintain, develop and renew (and not merely preserve) the social, economic and political order on the basis of values that are fundamentally derived from great religious traditions and human practice.

2.3 Cultivation and development of the physical well being of pupils.

2.4 Cultivation and development of the abilities of communicative competence both in spoken and written form and through a number of modes including verbal, numerical, mathematical and artistic.

2.5 Awareness of the interplay of performance and change in the social process so that the roots as described in A1 are maintained, but the tentative nature of human condition and interaction are also understood.

2.6 Knowledge of modern science and technology and an awareness and a critical understanding of their relationship to socio-cultural ethics and the fundamental values to which reference has been made in A2.

2.7 Mastery of scientific and other skills necessary for work and living in modern society.

Suggested guidelines for implementing these curriculum objectives

1. The aim is to equip growing young people with an inner understanding of the basic relation between knowledge and faith, knowledge and virtue, knowledge and action, knowledge and power, knowledge and wealth, knowledge and the socio-political environment and knowledge and national development, so that they may be able to choose to practise religion with an inner understanding of its spiritual, moral and material significance and act according to the religious criterion of conduct in the individual, social, national and international spheres of their existence, and feel a healthy normal satisfaction in being able intellectually to justify their practice in the light of human beings' relationship with God, other human beings and the natural world.

RELIGIOUS DIVERSITY IN SCHOOLS

Press coverage of events that involve a fundamental conflict between Islam and Western societies, including the Iranian revolution, the Rushdie controversy and various acts of terrorism, have contributed to the view that, within a larger post-cold war context, there is an underlying tension between Western and Islamic values (Esposito, 1995). This ideological clash is reflected in the media, through the press coverage of particular events, but also in education (Halstead, 1993). The schooling of Muslim children, particularly the display of their Islamic identity within the education system, has been perceived as problematic enough to become a focal point of public and media attention and there have been controversial debates in the press. Disputes range from state funding of denominational schools and religious education to religious symbols, praying and absences for religious reasons. The wearing of the Islamic headscarf in school and the state funding of Islamic schools are the most publicly disputed situations in French and British schools.

The Islamic headscarf was explicitly condemned as a symbol of backwardness and militancy, threatening the principle of laïcité, and the behaviour of the veiled Muslim schoolgirls was characterised as being aggressive, provocative and obstinate. In Britain the wearing of the headscarf in school was discussed in terms of school discipline, safety, discrimination and race relations, and was handled in a pragmatic manner. While in France the Islamic headscarf issue was debated in terms of religion and the principle of laïcité, in Britain the same question was also discussed in terms of discrimination and race and ethnic relations. Modesty in attire forms an important part of the dress code and although provision has been made for this in community schools there are still cases of Muslim girls being prevented from wearing the "hijab" or head covering. (Ameli *et al.*, 2004, Molokotos-Liederman, 2000).

Objection by schools to the wearing of the hijab has taken place in France and Germany because it has been seen as a political, as well as a religious symbol. The content analysis of the British newspaper articles on the school funding issue in Britain (Molokotos-Liederman, 2000) revealed that the debate was focused primarily on discrimination and religious education, viewed within the general context of British ethnic and race relations. The issue of equity and discrimination focused on the treatment of Muslim students relative to other religions, particularly to Judaism, and raised the question of why Islamic schools could not receive state funding when there was a significant number of Anglican, Roman Catholic and Jewish schools being funded (fully or partially) by the state. Furthermore, the argument of discrimination was carried further with the idea that existing British legislation on state funding of denominational schools is biased and particularly unfavorable to the start-up of small, low-budget schools, such as Islamic schools.

Despite the different nature of the two issues, one dealing with dress codes, the other with school funding, the two controversies, as debated in the national daily press raised the question of how to manage religious pluralism and balance diversity, unity and equality in education. Furthermore, the two case studies shared some common themes, namely, women's issues, particularly the status of women in Islam; discrimination issues specific to Islam, particularly when compared to Judaism; politically divisive elements in both debates; and concerns over the integration of Muslims.

METHODOLOGY AND SAMPLE GROUP

This report follows a sociological approach based on a questionnaire survey and qualitative interviews. The quantitative questionnaire was part of a major survey carried out by the IHRC and reported in the first volume of 'British Muslims' Expectations of the Government :Dual Citizenship: British, Islamic or both?' (Ameli & Merali, 2004) and the second volume of 'British Muslims' Expectations of the Government: Social Discrimination' (Ameli et al, 2004). A detailed description about participants and their demography has been offered in that report, here follows a summary. The total number of quantitative responses came to 1125, with some 800 being collated by hand, and the rest through a widely publicised on-line facility, over a three-week period. The majority of them are male (64%), with slightly over one-third female (36%). They are from diverse ethnic backgrounds, including South Asian, Mixed, Turkish, Iranian, Afro-Caribbean and English, and the level of their religiosity and identification with Islam is also diverse, ranging from devout practitioners to cultural and secular Muslims. About 90 percent of the participants are British citizens and more than half of them (55%) were born in Britain.

About 43 percent of the respondents are employed, while the rest of the participants fall into the categories of the unemployed, self-employed and students. The sample group includes respondents from England, Scotland and Wales; approximately half (47%) of them live in London.

We also interviewed 44 students in years 10-13 and 12 parents of children in these age ranges. Respondents came from across England, with several from London and others from Derby, Birmingham, Luton, Solihull, Winchester,

Tamworth, Oldham, Ilford, Brighton and other areas of England. The ethnic origins of interviewees were also diverse and included Pakistanis, Bangladeshis, English, Welsh, Mixed, Iraqi, Iranian, Kenyan, Yemeni and Gulf Arab respondents. These interviews helped us to interrogate the quantitative findings, as well as examine the complexity of preference and expectation within Muslim educational aspirations.

RESEARCH FINDINGS

The Islamic Human Rights Commission conducted a survey on British Muslims' Expectations and amongst 1125 Muslims, 47.5% would prefer to send their children to a Muslim school rather than a state school. 40% responded that their religious values were the greatest anxiety for them as their children grow up. 38.5% of respondents would choose the best school (regardless of whether it is mainstream or Muslim) and only 8.5% chose the option of a mainstream school.

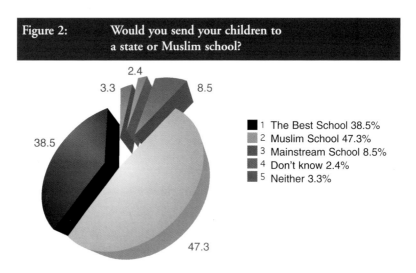

Figure 2: **Would you send your children to a state or Muslim school?**

2.4
3.3
8.5
38.5
47.3

1 The Best School 38.5%
2 Muslim School 47.3%
3 Mainstream School 8.5%
4 Don't know 2.4%
5 Neither 3.3%

The low preference of mainstream schools can also be witnessed nationally. It is not just the poor academic performance of their children that has led to many Muslim parents regarding the British education system as a failure. Muslim parents questioned the values being imparted in the state-school environment and whether there were aspects of disadvantage and discrimination that were affecting the children's capacity to build a positive sense of their identity. In addition to these problems the school social environment also caused concern to many Muslims, especially the harassment experienced by Muslim pupils.

Current political debate fostered by liberal and secular discourses in multi-culturalism (Ouseley 2001) and fuelled by highly politicised rhetoric (Bell, 2005) sets the desire for Islamic faith schools in direct contradiction to the values required in fostering a sense of citizenship amongst children, and indeed promoting segregation and thus the combined ills of ghettoisation and disaffection. Religion – in its ideological sense – and religiosity have been cast in the public debate as causes of these ills, and hence the desire for and expression of both by Muslims is seen as a negative social factor.

In the light of previous studies that have shown a sense of citizenship and religiosity as well as perceived religious requirement as highly compatible amongst Muslims (Ameli & Merali, 2004), this section explores further the role of Muslim education as an experience or aspiration in fostering the emotional and cognitive aspects of citizenship that create rounded and engaged citizens. It will also look at the factors responsible for creating a culture of (aspirational and actual) segregation i.e. ideological religiosity, social and economic disadvantage and experiences of discrimination and assesses how far these are justifiable explanations for this desire. In so doing it will assess whether an increasingly secularised mainstream educational system and an anti-faith school policy at governmental level are desirable or counterproductive to the project of social cohesion: whether the desire expressed by the respondents in the survey is for 'Muslim' educational space – what that represents in terms of mainstream and Muslim school experiences; why this desire should be so strong; what the 'best' school represents to Muslim parents; and why there is such a strong disinclination to what is (perceived to be) mainstream schooling. It will also look at the expectations and experiences of students (mainly) from year 10-13 and how these mirror or diverge from those of Muslim parents. It will further interrogate whether, as perceived by the mainstream, Muslims see Muslim educational space as an articulation of their perceived chauvinism, or whether they see it as part of a solution to existing problems within the mainstream.

SECULARITY AND THE DESIRE FOR MUSLIM SCHOOLS

Religiously orthodox elites are becoming increasingly aware that secularism threatens their social and political identities. Tariq Modood, a British Muslim, notes that "the real division of opinion is not between a conservative element in the Church of England versus the rest of the country, but between those who think religion has a place in secular public culture and those who think not" (Modood, 1994). Similarly, Leslie Newbigin, a British Christian asserts, 'in our present situation in Britain, where Christians and Muslims share a common position as minority faiths in a society dominated by the naturalistic ideology, we share a common duty to challenge this ideology' (Newbigin et al, 1998).

This was reflected in a number of parent responses and reflected a general concern amongst parents interviewed over the secular nature of mainstream education. When asked if there was a contradiction between secular education systems and religious values, parents overwhelmingly answered positively:

Yes. Secularism is often hostile to religion, and to a religious or spiritual outlook. So, one has to balance one's religious values against the dominating secularism that one finds today.

(Male 47, Cambridge)

Yes but I am realistic about what a secular system can offer and what it will be reluctant to offer. We try to fill the gaps at home.

(Male, 57, Solihull)

Yes, the secular system undermines religious beliefs.

(Male, 50, Cambridge)

Student responses fell into three distinct categories of equal weighting: those who saw no contradiction; those who were unsure or saw disparity and qualification according to schools and those who saw systemic differences. Those who saw no contradiction, rarely explained their response indicating, maybe, insufficient understanding of the systemic nature of the question. One respondent expressed his opinion thus:

> No, I think that religion promotes the gaining of knowledge in any way, so any education is good. Religion is not contradicted by education in any way.
>
> (Male, 15, London)

This is a well-known Islamic decree and is much used in Islamic teaching. This may account for the level of response combined with a lack of understanding of what a secular system of education may mean. In Volume 1 of this series, respondents defining their understanding of citizenship also had similar responses whereby they reflected a general misapprehension as to what citizenship may entail, seeing it as a legal formality with regard to passport holding. Others who saw citizenship in a more conceptual sense of rights and obligations, as well as affiliation and loyalty, saw in both qualitative responses and very high quantitative numbers[13] no contradiction between Islamic values and being a good British citizen. Student responses can be seen as mirroring both the levels of confusion as well as indignation at claims that tensions exist.

Some were able to articulate their uncertainty regarding any contradiction as based on the particularity of different schools that undermine the totality of what a secular education system in the UK may mean.

> As long as they provide prayer rooms and allow hijab etc., no.
>
> (Male, 19, London)

 Of those who saw contradictions, both devotional and curricular issues were cited:

> Yes, sometimes you are told to wear short skirts and short sleeved tops, which is against religion.
>
> (Female, 14, East Sussex)

> Yes, secular education rarely touches on religion let alone religious values.
>
> (Male, 18, Westminster)

> Secular systems believe that every individual should be the same; however it's a contradiction within itself because every individual is unique and comes from different background and faith groups. In secular system everyone has to dress the same, this is overtly targeting Muslims since we are the only religion that has a particular hijab conditions for girls to adhere to.
>
> (Female, 18, Brighton)

> Yes. Because my religion dictates certain etiquette which are not recognised within the secular education system at present, example of which are providing time for prayer; interaction between female and male are prescribed within my religion which are not also recognised in secular education system.
>
> (Female, 17, London)

It would follow, as Table 1 indicates, that those who perceive themselves to be highly practising Muslims would choose the option of Muslim schools over all others. Conversely, it would be assumed that increasing self-perceptions of secularity, low religiosity and cultural rather than ideological affiliation to Muslimness would produce the opposite result. However, given the choice between a mainstream school, a Muslim school, the best school or neither, those professing to be cultural Muslims and secular Muslims chose the 'best school' rather than a 'mainstream school' as their preferred choice. The second highest response in both categories was for Muslim schools at 30% and 31.25% respectively. This result was mirrored by those who said they did not know how religious they were with a much narrower margin between the figures of 33.3% favouring the best school and 28.8% favouring a Muslim school.

Table 1:	Level of Religiosity and School Preference amongst Muslims in Britain					
	Main-stream School	Muslim School	The Best School	Neither	Don't know	TOTAL
I don't know	4 6.1%	19 28.8%	22 33.3%	20 30.3%	1 1.5%	66 100.0%
Highly practicing Muslim	6 3.7%	104 64.2%	48 29.6%	4 2.5%	0 0.0%	162 100.0%
Practicing Muslim Count	50 7.0%	350 48.9%	287 40.1%	10 1.4%	19 2.7%	716 100.0%
Secular Muslim	19 24.7%	24 31.2%	31 40.3%	0 0.0%	3 0.3%	77 100.0%
Cultural Muslim	8 16.0%	15 30.0%	24 48.0%	1 2.0%	2 4.0%	50 100.0%
Don't care about Islamic Values at all	2 40.0%	0 0.0%	2 40.0%	0 0.0%	1 20.0%	5 100.0%
TOTAL	89 8.3%	512 47.6%	414 38.5%	35 3.3%	26 2.4%	1076 100.0%

Whilst ideological attachment to Muslim schools can be inferred from these results on the part of those who exhibit religiosity, the converse cannot be said of those with a more secular outlook. Indeed the categories of cultural and explicitly secular Muslims do not show a disinclination towards Muslim schools, and/or an ideological inclination towards mainstream schools, but rather a preference for the best school regardless of its faith base or lack thereof.

This indicates that even those Muslims, who see religion as a negligible, minor or marginal part of their lives and identities, see scope for the utility of faith-based education, and do not see necessary contradictions between their secularity and faith schooling. This is important when one considers the emphasis by those arguing against Muslim educational space from an ideologically secular perspective, as it undermines the polarity that their argument posit, and the implied incompatibility of secular education and Islamic values and Islamic education systems.

13

77.9% saw little or no contradiction between being a good British citizen and Islamic values, Ameli & Merali, *Dual Citizenship: British, Islamic or Both*, Islamic Human Rights Commission (2004)

EDUCATION SYSTEMS, CURRICULA AND MUSLIM SCHOOLING

In interviews, respondent parents expressed their disinclination towards secular mainstream schooling as a complex of concerns. Many themes recurred throughout responses. Lack of respect for religious values, either in the environment of their child's school, across the education system or in particular lessons, was a recurring concern and a source of contradiction for parents between their religious values and secular education. Darwinist theories and sex education were high amongst concerns.

> Yes. Biology. I believe some things about evolution is incorrect and feel that it contradicts the basic tenet of Islam. Generally OK.
>
> (Male, 45, Wembley)

> Yes, I do see contradictions between religious values and the content of lessons; sex education being on the top of my agenda. I have issues of sex being expended of young children in society at present. There is no teaching of sex in each religion and culture and the values of each religion/culture.
>
> (Female, 35, Wembley)

> Not at my child's school which is a Muslim school, but certainly when I was a student – particularly in terms of Darwinist theories. Concerns of an overbearing emphasis on this and other contradictory issues was a motivator in my sending my children to an Islamic school.
>
> (Female, 34, London)

> There are many aspects of the foundations upon which science is taught that contradict Islam. Only believe in what u can see, everything should be testable. Therefore god does not exist because we can't see him. The fact that because 'man' has 'found' or 'understood' how the world works, science is taught without recoginising everything has been created. Evolution is taught as fact young children can be confused because they look up to the teacher intellectually.

> Sex ed in biology is very graphic without any morals, rules or responsibility.
>
> (Female, 30, Ilford)

> Yes, especially sex education. It's the kind of things they teach at this age - not appropriate in our culture as it encourages pre-marital sex.
>
> (Male, 50, Cambridge)

> Yes. Biology. Sex education is included in biology in secondary school. My daughters attend an all girls school and this subject has been taught by male tutors much to the embarrassment of both female pupils and teacher alike. There is no relationship context to this subject and instruction is presented purely as a human/animal biological function. In addition the school puts on 'Brooke' counselling days which girls must attend and are given an absent mark if they do not turn up for these extra curricula programmes.

> Swimming and showers after PE. Some girls for a number of legitimate reasons do not feel comfortable with swimming even in an all girls' school. Pupils' attendance is checked and parents contacted if girls are found to be absent on swimming days.

Some PE teachers still insist on the ritual of showering after PE even though we are now living in an age where households have adequate access to bathing/showering/hot water etc in their own homes.

In both the above situations it appears that there is little thought given to natural feelings of modesty in young people (regardless of sex, racial or religious background)…

Art/Drama/Music. The children feel that some activities in these areas are questionable in terms of Islam, often there is a sense that tasks are frivolous or not conducive to Islamic etiquette e.g. one of my secondary school daughters was recently instructed to construct 3D Bra and knickers for an art project – despite her offer to construct some other 3D object

(Male, 57, Solihull)

Students also reflected some of these concerns to a lesser extent regarding mixing of the sexes, PE and dance classes, where there was lack of sensitivity towards personal beliefs in these areas:

RE. Biology – body cutting stuff unnecessary
(Male, 15, London)

Dancing, in PE, coloured scarves are not allowed.
(Female, 16, Wembley and Female, 15, Wembley)

RE/RS lessons were also singled out by some parents, with one 57 year-old male from Birmingham commenting that in RE, "Islam is often not taught sympathetically or objectively. Some RE teachers are still asking students to draw God." However, as evidenced above, many other lessons came under criticism as a source for conflict between students' religious values and the educational environment they were in. Sex education and PSHE lessons, as well as teachings of Darwinist theories were of most concern to parents. Whilst students interviewed did not share the same level of concern about systemic clashes between their cultural and religious values and the education system, they did express similar concerns about content of lessons. The concerns over lesson content were remarkably similar between parents and children.

Children particularly singled out Darwinist theory and the Big Bang theory as a source for concern:

Evolution.
(Male, 15, London)

Yes, theory of evolution in Biology
(Male, 14, Wembley)

Yes, especially in Bio as Darwin's theory is taught.
(Female, 16, East Ham)

Evolution, big bang theory, these are topics which are brought up whilst studying the subject
(Male, 18, London)

> Sometimes; in biology when taught the evolution theory and in physics when taught the big bang
>
> (Female, 14, East Sussex)

> Sometimes, in biology they emphasis a topic even when it is only theory.
>
> (Male, 16, Brighton)
>
> Only in Biology – Darwinian Theory but it is interesting to learn what the "other half" think.
>
> (Male, 19, London)

The Big Bang theory was also of concern, as one 18 year-old student attending an Islamic college in London stated: 'Evolution in Biology contradicts with our religious values. So does the Big Bang Theory. Basically, beliefs in our origin differ.'

According to our survey, of the half of respondents who saw a contradiction between what they learn in school and their cultural and educational values, only two saw the contradiction as a positive experience. However, both of them also have generally positive experiences of school based around strong anti-discrimination policies and high learning values (the implications of which will be discussed below):

> I believe that what is learnt in school is what is most to do with the country that it is taught in. For example, in history lessons people learn about British society over the years, and this is relevant to many people in the school. In this way, it is not a contradiction to some peoples' cultural values, just something that has to be put up with.
>
> (Male, 15, London)

> Any lesson in school which discusses or refers to cultural values usually includes most valid points of view. Naturally, some of those ideas are contradictory with my own values, but again, because so many different points of view are taught, it doesn't cause a problem.
>
> (Male, 15, Middlesex)

Again, the teaching of religious education was cited by students as a contradictory experience. Other subjects were also a cause of contradiction between the learning experience and students' values and underscores again a recurring concern amongst parents that mainstream schools are a space for cultural clash rather than cohesion:

> Sort of, things we learn in school are different to the way things are taught in families in our culture. At home our image and peoples judgment of us seems to be very important to parents and so in turn affects our actions. Whereas at school we are used to doing what we feel is right rather than what others will think of it.
>
> (Female, 17, Derby)

> Yes, if you are taught something then you are not told that this does not apply to your religion.
>
> (Female, 19, Brighton)

> When they talk about arranged marriages etc they stereotype it as a Muslim thing to do which is not true.
>
> (Female, 14, East Sussex)

Yes. If you follow culture, you are seen as 'backward.'

(Female, 17, London)

In terms of marriage culture and boyfriend/girlfriend.

(Female, 18, London)

Yes, because one time I got paired with a male.

(Female, Luton)

Yes – school teaches equal opportunities for all but culture (not Islam).

(Male, 18, Westminster)

Obviously my cultural values are different with the values existing in this country.

(Female, 16, London)

There has been a lack of respect to parents as in general. I have heard students swear the odds at their parents.

What I have also learnt in school is after your parents are of a certain age they belong to the nursing home and you wouldn't like to have any contact with them until their death.

(Female, 18, Brighton)

My culture comes from Islam things such as boys and girls socialising and dancing, undressing for pe together, music, non-Muslim festivals, sex-education, taking a non-Muslim as a role model the list is endless. These all contradict Islam therefore I do not want my children to find them acceptable.

(Female, 30, Ilford)

Sexual morality

(Male, 50, Cambridge)

…the perspectives, the outlooks are different and hence contradictions arise.

(Male, 43, Cambridge)

Of course there are constant contradictions between one's "cultural values" (religious, 'Eastern', ethnic, eg South Asian) and that which is taught at school (anti-religious, secularist, 'Western').

(Male, 47, Cambridge)

Whilst the parent responses go some way to explaining the large number of those surveyed who prefer Muslim schools, sophisticated analyses were also proffered by respondents who favoured mainstream schooling in principle but who saw lack of consistency and serious disparity within the mainstream. Even where obvious desires or expectations for faith schools as an alternative to mainstream education were not postulated, the desire for duality within the mainstream was expressed, not simply in terms of religious education but other relevant factors. One respondent advised:

If so many parents wish to educate their children at Muslim schools. This obviously means that the state schools are not providing or achieving the levels of achievement they want for their children. Religion might not be the only concern for sending a child to a Muslim school.

More research needs to be done on this subject and as to why exactly parents are choosing Muslim schools for their children. If their needs can be incorporated in the state schools than this should be encouraged rather than segregation in Muslim schools.'

(Female, 47, London)

These responses highlight concerns within this discourse about under-achievement of Muslim students, and the following section discuses how this may impact on the preferences of Muslim parents. Even as part of a main-stream solution, parents with a disinclination towards Muslim schools, argue for a recognition of the lack within the mainstream that disadvantages Muslim children, either directly impacting on their educational attainment or their and their non-Muslim peers' development into assured young adults.

Both parents and students saw distinctions between non-controversial subjects within the curricula e.g. most science, maths etc., whilst highlight-ing areas of cultural concern and conflict in some subjects e.g. PE, dance, music. Clearly both see large areas of coherence between their values and aspirations as well as conflict in a manner not dissimilar to other faith communities. A model of polycentric education for faith communities is effectively an aspiration for both those who desire Muslim schools as well as those who prefer or accept the mainstream.

MUSLIM EDUCATION AND SOCIAL & ECONOMIC DISADVANTAGE: CAUSES OR CURES?

Again, the desire for faith schooling is commonly attributed to social and economic disadvantage e.g. lower standards of education and low income. However, the survey showed that income or level of education were not over-whelmingly significant factors in the desire for Muslim schools. Whilst those with a higher income favoured 'the best school', lower and middle earners in the survey plumped for Muslim schools (See table 2).

Table 2:	Income and School Preference amongst Muslims in Britain					
	Main-stream School	Muslim School	The Best School	Neither	Don't know	TOTAL
Lower Class	13 4.5%	158 55.1%	94 32.8%	10 3.5%	12 4.2%	287 100.0%
Middle Class	75 10.0%	339 45.1%	302 40.2%	23 3.1%	13 1.7%	752 100.0%
Upper Class	1 2.6%	15 39.5%	19 50.0%	2 5.3%	1 2.6%	38 100.0%
TOTAL	89 8.3%	512 47.5%	415 38.5%	35 3.2%	26 2.4%	1077 100.0%

Likewise, more than half of those from Afro-Caribbean, Bangladeshi and Pakistani ethnic backgrounds chose Muslim schools as their preferred option, so too did those identifying themselves as White Muslims (see table 5). Indian and Arab Muslims, generally considered more affluent and well-educated, opted for the best school, but not in significantly greater numbers. East African Asians, considered more affluent and better educated, opted for

Muslim schools. One respondent of East African origin favoured mainstream schooling seeing her cultural values and morals being reflected in the grammar school of her son but not the comprehensive school of her daughter:

> I have a son at a single sex Grammar school which has very strict values and these values are enforced without exception. E.g. if a child is found to be in possession of drugs he is expelled. Code of behaviour and dress is rigidly enforced and so forth. So even though I have some reservations with this school (on racial grounds and that the school statistical data is put before the interest of the child). The general school ethos and cultural values are very much in tune with mine. This school realises that the education of a child is a school/parent job and the parents are very much consulted in the first few years and I also got good feedback e.g. if my child did not perform well or homework not done I was telephoned by the teacher with their concerns. (This is not the case with my daughter's comprehensive school)
>
> My daughter attends a comprehensive mixed school. Although it is one of the best comprehensive schools in the borough, their cultural values are not in tune with mine and consequently it makes my task of enforcing my values on my daughter difficult. I was not successful in getting her into a single sex school on religious grounds and since girls perform better in single sex schools this is of concern to me.
>
> (Female, 47, London)

This lack of values in parts of the mainstream appears from interviews to be a driving concern regardless of whether interviewees see the mainstream or Muslim schools as their preferred choice of school.

> I do not feel that the school policy in relation to what is expected of pupils and parents contradicts Islamic principles. However individual attitudes of some teachers/other staff/pupils may contradict those expectations. For example one RS teacher spent much of her class time chatting about boyfriends and wanting to buy a fast car etc.
>
> (Male, 57, Solihull)

Likewise, only those respondents with education at PhD level favoured 'the best school' over Muslim schools, with all other education levels, favouring Muslim schools (Table 3).

Table 3:	Level of Education and School Preference amongst Muslims in Britain					
	Main-stream School	Muslim School	The Best School	Neither	Don't know	TOTAL
Below GCSE	2 3.3%	30 49.2%	19 31.1%	8 13.1%	2 3.3%	61 100.0%
GCSE or Equivalent	16 8.2%	103 53.1%	67 34.5%	4 2.1%	4 2.1%	194 100.0%
A Level or Equivalent	19 8.5%	101 45.1%	94 42.0%	5 2.2%	5 2.2%	224 100.0%
Undergraduate	24 7.7%	159 51.0%	109 34.9%	11 3.5%	9 2.9%	312 100.0%
Postgraduate	26 10.1%	111 43.2%	109 42.4%	6 2.3%	5 1.9%	257 100.0%
PhD	2 6.9%	8 27.6%	17 58.6%	1 3.4%	1 3.4%	29 100.0%
TOTAL	89 8.3%	512 47.5%	415 38.5%	35 3.2%	26 2.4%	1077 100.0%

In comparison to the analysis of education in Volume 1 of this series with regard to feelings of citizenship and belonging, it was noticeable that the higher the level of education, the lower the level of satisfaction amongst British Muslims with Britain. Again, this challenges ideas of social disadvantage as a cause of either alienation or indeed a desire for 'ghettoisation'. Set in the context of a very highly educated sample preferring Muslim schools and then the best school (whether Muslim or not) over mainstream schools, this suggests conscious choices for Muslim educational space despite 'advantage'. The declining trend in preference for Muslim schooling as levels of education increase should be set off against the result of satisfaction within the same survey group. Less affiliation the idea of Muslim schools does not conversely mean support for the mainstream as these results variously show.

There was a positive correlation between higher levels of education and wanting the best school. A number of studies have suggested that education has a liberalising effect on political opinions (Jennings, M.K. and Niemi, R.G., 1981, *Generations and politics: A Panel Study of Young Adults and their Parents*. Princeton, NJ, Princeton University Press).

Some scholars have advocated multicultural education in West European countries on the ground that learning about other faiths would make people more tolerant and understanding of religious diversity (Nielsen, J.S., 1999, *Towards a European Islam*, London: Macmillan Press). Many Muslim parents saw as an ideal the possibility of Muslim schools being able to take on non-Muslim children and both pro-Muslim school and pro-mainstream parents expressed a concern that the teaching of students within the mainstream and Muslim schools should reflect better, accurate, fair and positive teaching of other cultures. Respondents' views indicate that they associate that pluralism with the Islamic values they see lacking in the education of their children within the mainstream system, and something that faith-based schooling can and should better address. Ironically, it is this sense of religious value that encourages this version of liberalism.

AGE AND EDUCATIONAL CHOICE

The responses received by all age ranges shed light on the multifaceted motivations for this, and are key to this analysis to avoid representing Muslims as ideologically aggressive to mainstream education.

Age grouping showed a significant difference between 15-19 year group and those aged 25 and over regarding the preference of Muslim schooling. The 30-34 age group showed the highest percentage preference of 61.2%.

Table 4:	Age Group and School preference among Muslims in Britain					
	Main-stream School	Muslim School	The Best School	Neither	Don't know	TOTAL
15-19	13 7.0%	70 37.8%	89 48.1%	7 3.8%	6 3.2%	185 100.0%
20-24	26 9.7%	119 44.4%	104 38.8%	8 3.0%	11 4.1%	268 100.0%
25-29	22 11.3%	101 52.1%	62 32.0%	6 3.1%	3 1.5%	194 100.0%
30-34	9 6.5%	85 61.2%	41 29.5%	2 1.4%	2 1.4%	139 100.0%
35-39	5 6.0%	45 54.2%	30 36.1%	2 2.4%	1 1.2%	83 100.0%
40-45	4 5.0%	45 56.3%	28 35.0%	1 1.3%	2 2.5%	80 100.0%
46-49	4 8.5%	18 38.3%	25 53.2%	0 0.0%	0 0.0%	47 100.0%
50 and above	13 10.1%	49 38.0%	54 41.9%	11 8.5%	2 1.6%	129 100.0%
TOTAL	96 8.5%	532 47.3%	433 38.5%	37 3.3%	27 2.4%	1125 100.0%

The lower preference amongst the very young may indicate a lack of life experience that informs their choice. Those respondents born outside Britain showed more preference towards Muslim schooling with 50.4% as compared to those born in Britain preferring Muslim schooling with 44.7%. Moreover, families from other countries do experience a culture clash which would affect their attitudes and choices.

Table 5:	Place of Birth and School preference amongst Muslims in Britain					
	Main-stream School	Muslim School	The Best School	Neither	Don't know	TOTAL
Britain	59 9.6%	275 44.7%	238 38.7%	22 3.6%	21 3.4%	615 100.0%
Other Countries	37 7.3%	257 50.4%	195 38.2%	15 2.9%	6 1.2%	510 100.0%
TOTAL	96 8.5%	532 47.3%	433 38.5%	37 3.3%	27 2.4%	1125 100.0%

The significance of the highest preference being in the 30-34 age range belies the thinking that preference is based on age and first generationalism. The 30-34 range is one where the majority of respondents are likely to have been born in the UK, and are reflecting troubling aspects of their own schooling in their choice:

> Sadly, the teaching cultures that I and my peers went through, although secular was very narrow in its mindset both towards people of other faiths and other ethnicities. Deliberate or not, many of us often felt we were belittled or considered backwards as a result of the way e.g. history portrays peoples of other cultures. Added to this I believe there is a general dislike towards religion that is shown time and again by teachers portraying those how are religious as defective. I was not a religious child, and neither were my family, however even then I felt that this was ridiculing others in an unfair and cruel way.
>
> (Female, 34, London)

> What is the purpose of a school within any ideological country? Every ideology wants every generation of children to be good citizens which will fit in and tow the line and believe and work for that systems. So the education system is a major part in producing such individuals. So the ideas that the society is built in will naturally be propagating and nurtured within the ed system. Hence in a secular capitalist society such as Britain, secularism. Freedom, multiculturalism, democracy are all pushed by the government. That is what I know is subtly and blatantly taught in schools. I have been to state school and I don't want my kids to gain the wrong ideas. I will explain these things to them and make sure they are not totally sheltered about these ideas but know how they are false. So I have very realistic expectations for the government and I will not send my kids to state school.
>
> (Female, 30, Ilford)

HIGHER ACHIEVEMENT AS A MOTIVATOR FOR MUSLIM SCHOOLS?

Achievement as a factor in choice of school informs the results significantly with the 'best school' topping responses in 4 categories, and coming second in the other two categories. The increasingly high achievement in league tables of Muslim schools also vindicated for many respondents the existence of Muslim schools as an environment that promotes learning and achievement as a result of its religious values.

Aside from the well-documented success of Feversham College in Bradford, a Muslim all-girls college that topped the 2004 'value added' league table in the UK, Muslim schools across the UK have been faring well in terms of academic results. According to the *Muslim News*, in 2004, the 5+ A*-C GCSE average pass rate of Muslim schools surpassed the national average by 3% (national average 54%, Muslim schools 57%). According to the paper's table, 52% of the Muslim schools featured attained higher A*-C pass rate than the national average with three attaining a 100% 5+ A*-C pass rate, including the Brondesbury School for Boys which also topped the league table for the London Borough of Brent. Additionally, the paper reports that:

"65% of the Muslim schools featured have a higher percentage of 5+ A*-C grades than their Local Education Authority average. Twenty three schools have a 100% 5+A*-G pass rate, whilst 61% of the schools featured in the table have had 100% of their students achieving at least 1 GCSE or GNVQ."[14] Additionally, the paper's research also finds that Muslim primary schools Key Stage 2 Level 4 (KS2L4) results are improving at a much higher rate than the National Average.[15]

This has obvious resonance with members of Muslim communities when, according to the national statistics in 2003-2004, almost a third (31%) of Muslims of working age in Great Britain have no qualifications – the highest proportion for any religious group. They are also the least likely to have degrees (or equivalent qualifications).[16]

The significance of this is threefold: the possibility of a Muslim school being a 'best school' belies the notion of religious schools being anathema to secular mindsets and values, particularly in terms of schooling; that achievement of schools rather than ideology is a motivating factor throughout the sample; Muslimness and Muslim educational space as part of a general discourse on good education are relevant and uncontentious factors for respondents regardless of their religiosity or secularity.

Table 4 shows the relationship between ethnic group and school preferences. There were no significant preferences between ethnic backgrounds. Respondents from Turkish backgrounds showed the lowest preference of 36.4% for Muslim schooling. Bangladeshi respondents showed the highest preference of 54.3% for Muslim schools followed by Pakistanis with 51.4%. This result is a reflection of concern arising from the unacceptably low academic attainment levels of many Muslim children.

---

[14] Elham Asaad Buaras, 'Muslim schools average beat national average' *The Muslim News*, http://www.muslimnews.co.uk/paper/index.php?article=1878, Issue 190, Friday 25 February 2005 - 16 Muharram 1426

[15] Elham Assad Buaras, 'Muslim primary schools achieving better than National Average' *The Muslim News*, http://www.muslimnews.co.uk/paper/index.php?article=1808, Issue 189, Friday 21 January 2005 - 10 Dhu al-Hijjah 1425

[16] http://www.statistics.gov.uk/cci/nugget.asp?id=963

Table 6:	Relations between Ethnic Group and School preference among Muslims in Britain					
	Main-stream School	Muslim School	The Best School	Neither	Don't know	TOTAL
Pakistani	36 9.4%	196 51.4%	129 33.9%	8 2.1%	12 3.1%	381 100.0%
Indian	18 6.7%	111 41.4%	124 46.3%	11 4.1%	4 1.5%	268 100.0%
Bangladeshi	4 4.3%	51 54.3%	31 33.0%	4 4.3%	4 4.3%	94 100.0%
Arab	6 6.8%	39 44.3%	37 42.0%	4 4.5%	2 2.3%	88 100.0%
Afro-Caribbean	0 0.0%	5 50.0%	3 30.0%	2 20.0%	0 0.0%	10 100.0%
White British	4 10.0%	20 50.0%	13 32.5%	2 5.0%	1 2.5%	40 100.0%
Turkish	0 0.0%	4 36.4%	6 54.5%	1 9.1%	0 0.0%	11 100.0%
Iranian	1 6.7%	6 40.0%	7 46.7%	0 0.0%	1 6.7%	15 100.0%
Mixed	5 14.3%	14 40.0%	15 42.9%	1 2.9%	0 0.0%	35 100.0%
Other	21 12.1%	82 47.1%	66 37.9%	2 1.1%	3 1.7%	174 100.0%
East African Asian	1 11.1%	4 44.4%	2 22.2%	2 22.2%	0 0.0%	9 100.0%
TOTAL	96 8.5%	532 47.3%	433 38.5%	37 3.3%	27 2.4%	1125 100.0%

Research from as early as the 1970s indicated that in some schools at least Muslim children from a variety of ethnic backgrounds performed less well than whites. Anwar found that the low achievers were children of those Pakistanis who worked odd hours and night shifts and so were unable to pay much attention to their children's needs. (Anwar, 1979)

In 1983, 27% of Pakistanis and 51% of Bangladeshis possessed no formal qualifications. In 1985 the Swann Committee observed that in a majority of schools it visited, 'there was a strong feeling that these pupils (Pakistanis and Bangladeshis) were underachieving' and the Turkish Cypriots were singled out as giving particular cause for concern. (p. 687)

Again, the relatively low variation between ethnic groups suggests a pan-Muslim consciousness regarding the utility of Muslim schools within the British context, and could suggest that the failures of the mainstream to address under achievement amongst ethnic groups through a thorough examination of its systemic failures is a concern that parents feel can no longer be addressed within the mainstream, and thus look towards schools that can create a normative environment that they and their children can relate to and therefore work, study and achieve within.

CREATING CONFIDENT INDIVIDUALS

School preference could also be a result of the attitudes, values and behaviour of teachers and schools affecting the way Muslim pupils saw themselves. Lack of individual attention, minimal praise and fewer opportunities to contribute to classroom discussion undermined self-confidence and in turn adversely affected educational attainment. The evidence in the 1990s suggested that teachers' attitudes had changed little (Eade, 1997:19).

Parent and student respondents identified a series of incidents in their personal experience that underscores (a) culture(s) of insensitivity and even hostility against Muslims. Some responses are truly shocking when interviewees were asked if they had any negative experiences with teaching staff, governors and in the case of students, peers, at school. Students responding in the affirmative made up half of all student interviewees – the highest negative response in any category where they were interviewed. These range from outright racism or Islamophobic discrimination to feelings of devaluation as a result of class discussions.

> There were some times during religious studies lessons where I doubted some of my religious values and during class discussions I felt that the teacher was giving biased views.
>
> (Female, 16, London)

> Students yes, because although the school do teach religion they don't give both sides.
>
> (Female, 14, East Sussex)

> The teachers, different ideas of religion.
>
> (Male, 16, Brighton)

> Yes. I found certain ignorance and naïve prejudice towards my religion with regards to state of woman in my religion amongst other things.
>
> (Male, 17. Winchester)

> Occasionally my values have been misunderstood or questioned, but large problems have rarely been caused.
>
> (Male, 15, Middlesex)

> Yes. One time my teacher said why do you Muslim girls always have to be so covered up and said "Why don't you take off your long coats".
>
> (Female, Luton)

> Yes sometimes I Hear groups of people mocking My god Allah
>
> (Male, 14, Greater Manchester)

> Yes, one teacher made me hold a boy's hand against my choice of Islamic value.
>
> (Male, 18, London)

> One... teacher didn't like me and boy Muhammad... Kept getting us in trouble – victimising.
>
> (Male, 15, London)

> Many teachers are racist, for us being Muslims, and the country we are from etc. Iraq, Palestine, treats you different from the others.
>
> (Female, 16, Wembley and Female, 15, London)

Indirectly many times. Teacher picks on me for what I believe.

(Male, Wembley)

Yes an R.E. teacher once mocked Shiaism as being a religion which cries for something that happened 1400 years ago. Totally devalued my religion and its values.

(Female, Luton)

So far no, however on a course for medical work experience at Nottingham one teacher suggested that if I can't place the stethoscope in my ear because of my scarf I should re-think my career in medicine.

(Female, 18, Brighton)

Yes! Teachers taking sides of whites.

(Male, 19, London)

Interestingly, most parents expressed some experiences, but some saw this as part of the course within the mainstream or were unsure as to its existence, sensing implicit problems:

Prejudice of some sort is always there.

(Male, 43, Cambridge)

No direct discrimination. Staff etc generally supportive.

(Male, 47, Cambridge)

I think so – but it is difficult to know for sure.

(Male, 57, Solihull)

...I think the discrimination is rather more based on race than religion (though I could be wrong – one can never be sure of why there is discrimination). However I do not let this have a negative effect on my communication with the school or the child.

(Female, 47, London)

General difficulties as a result of lack of understating of Muslim culture were also frequently cited as a cause of dysfunction in parent-school relationships:

School assemblies require our children to sing songs that hold no meaning for my child. I have objected to this. Drinks being offered at staff parties without consideration to Muslim parents/staff.

(Female, 35, Wembley)

This response is typical of the concerns Muslim parents expressed.

Discrimination as a factor, and the consequent undermining of identity was expressed by some parents and this concern seemed underscored by the large response from students evidencing negative experiences within the school setting. The effects of discrimination on preference for Muslim schooling is shown in Table 7

Table 7:	Experience of Discrimination and School Preference amongst Muslims in Britain					
	Main-stream School	Muslim School	The Best School	Neither	Don't know	TOTAL
I don't know	3 4.9%	21 34.4%	16 26.2%	21 34.4%	0 0.0%	61 100.0%
Almost Daily	1 1.2%	61 71.8%	20 23.5%	0 0.0%	3 3.5%	85 100.0%
Weekly	3 3.5%	46 53.5%	29 33.7%	2 2.3%	6 7.0%	86 100.0%
Monthly	5 6.1%	40 48.8%	36 43.9%	0 0.0%	1 1.2%	82 100.0%
Only on some occasion	49 8.2%	288 48.1%	243 40.6%	10 1.7%	9 1.5%	599 100.0%
Not at all	28 17.2%	56 34.4%	70 42.9%	2 1.2%	7 4.3%	163 100.0%
TOTAL	89 8.3%	512 47.6%	414 38.5%	35 3.3%	26 2.4%	1076 100.0%

Whilst acknowledging (in the context of Bradford) that Islamophobia was prevalent in schools and the community, Sir Herman Ouseley (2001) indicted ethnically homogenous schools and his critique was used to indict (the aspiration) for faith schools as evidenced:

> "Self-segregation…driven by fear of others, the need for safety from harassment and violent crime and the belief that it is the only way to promote , retain and protect faith and cultural identity and affiliation."

Whilst this explanation offers causality for such aspirations, this is not reflected across our survey. Respondents, who saw a Muslim school as the ideal environment for their children, often expressed the desire for such schools to be inclusive of others, and where an effective sense of citizenship could be encouraged in students:

Table 2 sees five survey areas where 50% or more of the respondents favoured Muslims schools, if given the choice, for their children. Of these Bradford is but one, suggesting that Ouseley's analysis carries some weight. However, beyond the specificity of the Bradford context, the assumption that the desire for single faith schools is driven in large part by experiences of discrimination is undermined. London reported a lower than average level of Islamophobic discrimination in the survey at 76.6 per cent, while Bradford reported a higher rate at 86.2 per cent. Of the two, Bradford had a significantly higher proportion of reports of people experiencing Islamophobia on a daily or weekly basis, 37.9 per cent compared to 13.6 per cent in London. Yet the aspiration for Muslim schools in both was almost identical - 53.4per cent in Bradford and 52.7 per cent in London. Slough, whose respondents showed the highest desire for Muslim schools according to locality (57 per cent) reported no experiences of Islamophobia on a daily or weekly basis, but only on some occasions (96.4 pre cent).[17]

---

[17]

For full results on the experience of Islamophobia see Volume 2 *Social Discrimination: Across the Muslim Divide* Ameli S.R., Elahi M, & Merali A., Islamic Human Rights Commission, (London, 2004)

Table 8:	Area of Residence and School Preference amongst Muslims in Britain					
	Main-stream School	Muslim School	The Best School	Neither	Don't know	TOTAL
Swansea	0 0.0%	5 50.0%	4 40.0%	0 0.0%	1 10.0%	10 100.0%
London	44 8.2%	282 52.7%	183 34.2%	15 2.8%	11 2.1%	535 100.0%
Birmingham	3 5.2%	27 46.6%	21 36.2%	5 8.6%	2 3.4%	58 100.0%
Manchester	7 19.4%	10 27.8%	18 50.0%	0 0.0%	1 2.8%	36 100.0%
Bradford	6 10.3%	31 53.4%	18 31.0%	0 0.0%	3 5.2%	58 100.0%
Glasgow	0 0.0%	4 44.4%	4 44.4%	1 11.1%	0 0.0%	9 100.0%
Newcastle	0 0.0%	2 20.0%	6 60.0%	2 20.0%	0 0.0%	10 100.0%
Cardiff	2 18.2%	3 27.3%	5 45.5%	1 9.1%	0 0.0%	11 100.0%
Oldham	2 14.3%	4 28.6%	4 28.6%	4 28.6%	0 0.0%	14 100.0%
Other	23 10.0%	94 40.9%	102 44.3%	5 2.2%	6 2.6%	230 100.0%
Coventry	0 0.0%	4 40.0%	6 60.0%	0 0.0%	0 0.0%	10 100.0%
Gloucester	1 2.4%	16 39.0%	23 56.1%	1 2.4%	0 0.0%	41 100.0%
Slough	0 0.0%	16 57.1%	10 35.7%	0 0.0%	2 7.1%	28 100.0%
Peterborough	1 3.7%	14 51.9%	11 40.7%	1 3.7%	0 0.0%	27 100.0%
TOTAL	89 8.3%	512 47.5%	415 38.5%	35 3.2%	26 2.4%	1077 100.0%

Whilst Table 3 shows clear correlations between the experience of discrimination and the desire for Muslim schools, Table 2 suggests that the importance of this result should not be exaggerated, and more sophisticated analyses sought. The desire for Muslim schools in this context is not necessarily a negative one fuelled by injustice or a self-fulfilling expectation of threat from majority society. The choice for Muslim schools seems to be a choice *for* something and not *against* 'secular', 'White', 'Christian' etc. education per se.

CREATING RELIGIOUS SPACE AND NURTURING SPIRITUALITY

A by-product of the 'self-segregation' argument is the desire to 'protect faith and culture'. This is by no means attributed solely to Muslims, but is seen as a negative and potentially chauvinistic practice in liberal and also, importantly, current policy discourse (Bell, 2005). This belies inherently prejudicial representations of religion per se. Parekh's (2000) description of race relations bodies depicts the pervasiveness of secularism and its effect on religiously defined identities and communities:

> "…most race equality organisations are broadly secular, not religious. It is perhaps for this reason that they frequently appear insensitive to forms of racism that target aspects of religious identity. For example, they are widely perceived by British Muslims to be insensitive to distinctive Muslim concerns, by Jewish people to be uninterested in anti-Semitism, and by Irish people to be indifferent to sectarianism and anti-Catholicism… there is little recognition … of the work and importance of black-majority churches."

This is a concern reflected in the aspirations of Muslim parents. There is a tendency for contemporary school life becoming colonised by a hegemony of performance indicators and it is likely, therefore, that the spaces for spiritual reflection and development are being reduced.

The nurture of the spiritual has never been straightforward but contemporary conditions in school and society appear to make it even more problematic. Gallagher, M.P. (1997, pp. 28-9) identifies the growing significance of 'secular marginalisation', a cultural phenomenon in which religion is not vigorously attacked by rationalist or atheist critics but rather simply ignored. From this perspective, secular marginalisation in the wider society begins to permeate the culture of faith-based schools. The serious nurture of the spiritual needs pro-tected by time and space, over and against the relentless pressure of educational performance efficiency has to be considered. The possibility that has to be faced and addressed is that spiritual development, although not quantified and entered on performance league tables, might become a marginalised and weaker sector of a school's activities.

In interviews, both parents and students within the mainstream whether in favour, against or ambivalent towards the idea of faith schools, emphasised the need for religious space within mainstream education systems when asked about the ideal school they desire for their children:

> High levels of education combined with Muslim cultural and religious values. An environment free of bullying and discrimination.
>
> (Male, 47, Cambridge)

> An inclusive 'Islamic' school. A school that in addition to teaching Islam and other subjects within an Islamic ethos that reflected the values generally expected within mainstream Islam it would also have to be comfortable about including all members and sectors of the Muslim (and non-Muslim) community. I would not feel happy in a school that reflected one particular ethnic or racial group or only one particular view of Islam. Ideally an Islamic school should reflect the diversity of the Ummah.

> Given that we are living in a multi-cultural and multi-faith com-munity an Islamic school needs to work on teaching pupils how to conduct themselves within such a society and the wider world and to give then sound instruction that would enable them to safeguard their faith.
>
> (Male, 57, Solihull)

> An ideal school for my children would be a school of my religion that would express different cultures and religions. This school would be governmental.
>
> (Female, 39, London)

I think it would be one where there is a strong ethos (preferably Islamic) which encourages self-confidence in pupils without being dogmatic. Although my ideal environment would be for an Islamic school, I would hope that there would be pupils from all backgrounds and faiths (or none) benefiting from this.

(Female, 34, London)

Independent Muslim school, run and funded by Muslims. No interference from government Ofsted is fine because that is about standards of building and teaching but curriculum and especially religious ed cannot be dictated. I thank Allah that my son goes to one such school Islamic Shaksiya Foundation in Walthamstow. It would be nice if the school was local but that's a price we are willing to pay for the sake of our kids and to fulfil our responsibility.

(Female, 30, Ilford)

Multicultural with multi-faith education and clear moral and religious education.

(Male, 40, London)

One where she can learn about all cultures and learn extensively about her own. P.E and swimming – offers female educators. Biology, chemistry – female educators. One she can proudly bring her beliefs and values into freely and be welcomed for her contribution.

(Female, 35, Wembley)

Halal food, prayer rooms and uniforms sympathetic towards Muslim dress codes are seen as essential components of an inclusive mainstream educational system, particularly amongst students. The failure to provide these were identified with other exclusionary factors e.g. the zealous promotion of Darwinist theories as undermining student confidence in the mainstream. Many felt that Muslims in mainstream syllabi fared ill e.g. in history they were generally portrayed as antagonists to a progressive European culture; their religion was portrayed as alien to European religious traditions, and their contribution to science, maths and the arts bypassed as practically non-existent.

As in Volume 1, these were recurring themes and common aspirations linked inextricably with a sense of what a better and inclusive society for all should look like. Addressing the prevailing culture where minority rights guaranteed through differential treatment are looked as favours and not prerequisites to equality, is part of the underlying discourse in these responses and corresponds as noted in Volume 1 as consistent with Addis' (1996) and Parekh's (Parekh et. al, 2000) contentions regarding the precursory requirements for the achievement of a multicultural form of citizenship. Put simply, an aspirationally plural society can only be created through the education of its next generation in a manner that guarantees their and their parents' rights to educational choice that reflects the particularity of minority identities alongside what is recognisably secular aspects of the mainstream educational curricula.

Without this combination of universalised aspects of curricula e.g. maths and non-ideologised science, and the respect for particularity of faith communities, the effects of discrimination and denial of minority rights coupled with negative stereotyping of faith communities within curriculum subjects, creates an unintentional but deeply-felt sense of humiliation within a school setting, where Muslims are implicitly learners further down an educational teleology than their non-Muslim/European peers. In other words, they are considered backward.

Misconceptions and perceptions of peers and teachers feature heavily in the experiences of those who had found that their faith had been devalued in a school environment, indicating a worrying level of Islamophobia and racism within schools.

> Yes. Following the event of September 11 have found people to be hostile to myself simply because they perceive me as a potential threat to life as we know it.
>
> (Male, 17, Winchester)

> By teachers putting you down for your language, and for being a Muslim.
>
> (Female, 16, Wembley and Female, 15, Wembley)

> Indirectly, yes.
>
> (Male, Wembley)

> Bullying experienced at _____ _____ [18]
>
> (Male, 19, London)

Whilst the majority of students belied the concern of their parents as regards bullying, those who claimed they had not experienced bullying gave a number of unexpected reasons for this. The multiculturalism of the area they live in and the mixed nature of the school rather than the school ethos was cited by one 15 year-old male in London: 'I do not feel isolated or muted in school because there are many Muslims in my school and I have experienced no bullying.' Conversely, the sense of leaving such a place emphasises difference and causes feelings of isolation:

I feel isolated, because I came from a rich multi-faith and multicultural place like London to a less multicultural/faith place like Brighton. In my school I am the only Muslim and hijab wearing person, however I have never experienced bullying in any form towards me or my faith, but that could be because I am not an easy target.

(Female, 18, Brighton)

No bullying but I feel isolated.

(Male, 16, Brighton)

All respondents from Muslim schools answered in the negative with some articulating clearly that the reason they were not muted or isolated stemmed from the nature of the school as 'Islamic':

> No, as I attend an Islamic college.
>
> (Male, 18, Westminster)

---

[18]

Name of school removed.

Others gave the reason for lack of bullying or feelings of isolation as a result of their own personality traits, formed at home and not at school:

> Never, I think my confidence has more to do with my upbringing than anything else.
>
> (Female, 17, Derby)

Other respondents, while answering negatively, did state that they felt they were asked to explain themselves or their faith. This in itself is an indicator of structural prejudice (Runnymede 1997).

> I don't feel left out, I do get questions but not bullying.
>
> (Female, 14, East Sussex)

> In my school I feel as if I am asked to explain myself more often than I am muted. I have never experienced bullying as a direct result of my faith, but a misconception of my religion and principles can lead people to be slightly more hesitant towards you.
>
> (Male, 15, Middlesex)

Both parents and students reflected this anxiety, which in some cases also manifested itself in feelings of depression and alienation. It can also lead to underachievement and the need for countering this as an aspirational goal for Muslim parents is validated by research from the 1970s when it became apparent to the members of the Turkish Muslim community and to British educationalists that even second generation Turkish children, who were born in Britain, were not only underachieving in British schools, but were also growing up in a different culture, ignorant of their own culture, language, religion and tradition, and becoming strangers to their own ethnicity and religion.

This, combined with a general sense of antipathy towards religious spirituality, alienates Muslim students from their peers and indeed educators, as perpetually and immutably 'other'. Respondents identified their spiritual values as being akin to mainstream morality currently absent in a systematic or meaningful way from secular education systems. Its much lamented loss was cited as detrimental not just to the development of believers within a particular faith system, but to society as a whole by the loss of confidence and thus viable and engaged future citizens.

INCULCATING CITIZENSHIP AND MUSLIM EDUCATIONAL SPACE

Many respondents described their aspirations for Muslim schooling in terms that vindicate the idea of Muslim educational spaces that allow the development of minority children in a religiously-founded identity of their parents' choosing, rather than a knee-jerk or unsophisticated reaction to discrimination. This desire is compounded in many cases by the idea of character building, not only in a religious or moral developmental way, but also in terms of civic awareness.

Many respondents saw Muslim schools as an ideal project where, if realised, values of good citizenship could be inculcated not only in Muslim children, but also in non-Muslim children. There was a strong articulation of dis-satisfaction with mainstream schooling in inculcating civic values amongst children. Many saw these values as best nurtured through religious schooling both currently and in an ideal setting:

> A school where my child will be able to be educated as a responsible Muslim British citizen without any fear and without any compromise of their identities.
>
> (Male, 38, Tamworth)

This trend adds credence to the potentiality of conflict resolution between communities through the development of dual education systems.

Others saw differences within the mainstream system between those that were able to provide such a safe and Islamic environment and those who were conspicuously failing to do so.

Whilst the tendency in public discussions has been to cast faith schools as divisive, many respondents saw their role in an ideal scenario as facilitating the exact opposite. When asked whether their children felt isolated, parents of children within Muslim schools universally said no. Of those who saw a Muslim school as an ideal, several indicated that this meant for them teaching diversity as well as allowing diversity within a general Islamic framework of education. One parent whose children had previously attended an Islamic school but were now in the state sector picked up on the possibility of Muslim schools replicating some of the failings within the mainstream regarding diversity when explaining his ideal school:

> An inclusive 'Islamic' school. A school that in addition to teaching Islam and other subjects within an Islamic ethos that reflected the values generally expected within mainstream Islam it would also have to be comfortable about including all members and sectors of the Muslim (and non-Muslim) community. I would not feel happy in a school that reflected one particular ethnic or racial group or only one particular view of Islam. Ideally an Islamic school should reflect the diversity of the Ummah.
>
> Given that we are living in a multicultural and multi-faith community an Islamic school needs to work on teaching pupils who conduct themselves within such a society and the wider world and to give them sound instruction that would enable them to safeguard their faith.
>
> (Male, 57, Solihull)

Others were equally keen to emphasise diversity:

> I think it would be one where there is a strong ethos (preferably Islamic) which encourages self-confidence in pupils without being dogmatic. Although my ideal environment would be for an Islamic school, I would hope that there would be pupils from all backgrounds and faiths (or none) benefiting from this.
>
> (Female, 34, London)

This was often compounded by experiences which saw the recognition of faith schools or mainstream schools with a large Muslim population.

Ideal scenarios for respondents included allowing more state funded Muslim schools, with existing private Muslim schools being allowed to move into the state sector. When asked if this was an ideal scenario most parents responded positively, regardless of whether they wanted to have a child in a Muslim school or not. Their reasons varied. A surplus of Muslim faith schools would allow for a much desired Muslim educational space that provides the same benefits to non-adherents, as well as addressing resource crises in Muslim schools. Further it would mark out equality between minorities:

> Yes, I do think private Muslim schools should be allowed to move into the state sector. This possibility will improve attitudes of Muslims and this would mix different religions and cultures.
>
> (Female, 39, London)

> Yes. Why not. They teach the same syllabus plus added things for Muslims.
>
> (Male, 50, Wembley)

> This is wishful thinking. I would like to see this happen as long as the school offers a broad curriculum and addresses British society and its values so our children are aware it exists.
>
> (Female, 34, Wembley)

> Yes they should. If so many parents wish to educate their children at Muslim schools. This obviously means that the state schools are not providing or achieving the levels of achievement they want for their children. Religion might not be the only concern for sending a child to a Muslim school.
>
> (Female 47, London)

Possibly. It'll address the resource problems that Islamic schools are facing at the moment.

(Male, 38, Tamworth)

More than ideal.

(Female, 34, London)

Why not? Yes, certainly a possibility. Muslims ought to have the same freedom in this matter as everyone else.

(Male, 47, Cambridge)

However, respondents in favour and against the move to the state sector raised issues about state interference in curricula as a result of state funding:

Yes. How this is handled in terms of state interference in the curriculum will have to be considered by those individual schools.

(Male, 57, Solihull)

The minute you take money from the state the state will interfere and start dictating to you what to teach and how you run the school. I have seen it happen with my own eyes. The Muslim community has been blessed with wealth. They should be more enlightened in their thinking about the consequences of taking state money.

(Female, 30, Ilford)

There were positive correlations between sense of belonging to Britain as the national space of life and preference for Muslim schooling, however again there were low levels of preference for mainstream schooling. As sense of belonging decreased, preference for Muslim schools increased. Table 9 shows the relationship between sense of belonging and schooling. Of those who felt a strong sense of belonging and a sense of belonging, 36.3% and 50.2% preferred the best school respectively.

Table 9:	Relations between sense of Belonging and Schooling among Muslims in Britain					
	Main-stream School	Muslim School	The Best School	Neither	Don't know	TOTAL
Yes, Very Strong	31 23.0%	50 37.0%	49 36.3%	3 2.2%	2 1.5%	135 100.0%
Yes, I feel a sense of belonging	40 12.4%	111 34.4%	162 50.2%	3 0.9%	7 2.2%	323 100.0%
Neutral	19 6.6%	128 44.8%	128 44.8%	6 2.1%	5 1.7%	286 100.0%
No, Not at all	1 0.6%	127 77.0%	32 19.4%	2 1.2%	3 1.8%	165 100.0%
No, I don't feel a sense of belonging	2 1.4%	90 61.6%	46 31.5%	0 0.0%	8 5.5%	146 100.0%
I don't know	3 4.3%	26 37.1%	16 22.9%	23 32.9%	2 2.9%	70 100.0%
TOTAL	96 8.5%	532 47.3%	433 38.5%	37 3.3%	27 2.4%	1125 100.0%

Again, these results are interrogated by response regarding respect for British law. Those who had no idea of their position with regard to British law showed a preference for the best school and then only by a small fraction of the category of 'neither' school and 'Muslim school'. According to table 10, those who showed full respect for British law actually preferred Muslim schools, and those with a religious sense of devotion to British law (they support British laws because it is a religious commandment to obey it) actually show priority for those schools which have the highest educational standards (Best School). Those with conditional or low levels of respect for British law showed a more marked preference for Muslim schools. This indicates that when feelings of marginalization become stronger, the demand for an 'indigenous minority culture' comes to play a central part of social and individual life.

Table 10:	Level of Respect for British Law and School Preference					
	Main-stream School	Muslim School	The Best School	Neither	Don't know	TOTAL
I have no idea	5 7.2%	20 29.0%	22 31.9%	21 30.4%	1 1.4%	69 100.0%
Yes, I respect all British Laws	35 15.2%	103 44.6%	87 37.7%	3 1.3%	3 1.3%	231 100.0%
I respect all British laws because of my religious values	41 11.5%	136 38.3%	166 46.8%	5 1.4%	7 2.0%	355 100.0%
I respect British law unless it interferes with my religious practice	14 3.2%	255 57.7%	152 34.4%	7 1.6%	14 3.2%	442 100.0%
I don't respect British Law at all	1 3.6%	18 64.3%	6 21.4%	1 3.6%	2 7.1%	28 100.0%
TOTAL	**96 8.5%**	**532 47.3%**	**433 38.5%**	**37 3.3%**	**27 2.4%**	**1125 100.0%**

Arguably the addressing of core issues identified as barriers to that respect, as well as creating dual educational spaces within the mainstream is a way of tackling the negativity associated with this result – one of the few where a negative correlation i.e. greater desire on the basis of less respect for the law, is so distinct.

Gender was a factor that showed a slight difference between preferring Muslim schooling to mainstream schooling with 42.9% preferring Muslim schooling from a total 401 female respondents. 49.7% male respondents preferred Muslim schools from a total of 724.

Table 11:	Gender and School preference amongst Muslims in Britain					
	Main-stream School	Muslim School	The Best School	Neither	Don't know	TOTAL
Female	43 10.7%	172 42.9%	167 41.6%	11 2.7%	8 2.0%	401 100.0%
Male	53 7.3%	360 49.7%	266 36.7%	26 3.6%	19 2.6%	724 100.0%
TOTAL	**96 8.5%**	**532 47.3%**	**433 38.5%**	**37 3.3%**	**27 2.4%**	**1125 100.0%**

Gender has been a factor that might help explain public attitudes toward state accommodation of Muslim religious practices in Western Europe. From the standpoint of some feminists, particularly in a populist setting, the Islamic faith is seen to be oppressing women in various ways. They claim that certain passages from the Qur'an teach the inferiority of women and that practices in some Muslim countries oppress women. What is beyond dispute is that the role of women in Islam is a highly contested issue in Western Europe. Muslim women declare that the Qur'an preaches the spiritual equality of women and men, and that Islam has achieved far more for women's emancipation and equality than what many of today's feminists realise. It is only Islam that has lifted women from the abyss of oppression to previously unknown levels of freedom which are unmatched even in today's so-called 'civilised' world.

Yet, any effort to retain a sense of modesty is immediately labelled 'oppressive', despite the protestation of the leaders of 'Islamist' discourses on an international stage, and academics trying to understand Muslim female practice such as the hijab. Fada Al-Guindi in 'Veil, modesty, privacy and resistance' asserts that 'the voluntary wearing of the hijab since the mid-seventies is about liberation from imposed, imported identities, consumerist behaviours and resisting…Western dominance.' (al-Guindi, 1999:184). The late Imam Khomeini said, "In the course of the revolution, women in our society have proved that they can serve Islam and Muslims alongside men, even in social and political activities and be vanguards in educating the esteemed society."

Fetzer and Soper (2003) concluded that women in Britain, France and Germany do not generally oppose state accommodation of Islam and they suggested that they are just as likely to accept the claims of many Muslim women as thy are to believe non-Muslim feminists on gender rights.

EXPECTATIONS OF THE GOVERNMENT

Given the preference for Muslim schooling, Muslim parents in their expectations of the government looked to more traditional and tangible results, ranging from better standards to equal opportunities for minorities in mainstream schools and better anti-discrimination measures:

> I expect the schools to be funded better and to ensure that we have better quality teachers available. At the moment very few maths teachers have a math degree as their qualification. I realise that not all schools can be grammar schools however if just the cultural values and attitudes of my son's grammar school could be adopted in comprehensive schools there would be a major improvement in comprehensive schools. Also there is a big problem of disruptive students who do not allow learning to take place in lessons. The government needs to deal with this problem more effectively.

> I wish there were more single sex schools and it should be a matter of choice rather than places available if parents wish to send their children to single sex school.
>
> (Female, 47, London)

> My expectations are to improve the number of schools in a particular borough as well as of good education.
>
> (Female, 39, London)

I hope that they take into account everyone's religious belief and cultural background when they design the curriculum.

(Male, 50, Wembley)

Government needs to focus on individuals when it comes to religious/social cultural values and educate accordingly. This is to stop confusion in children that are anything other than Christian. This should cover equal opportunities.

(Female, 34, Wembley)

The system fails to properly fulfil the needs of the ethnic minorities. Adequate resources need to be made available.

(Male, 50, Cambridge)

To enable children to perform their best to their ability despite race, religion, and colour.

(Male, 43, Cambridge)

Schooling system should recognise the religious identities of their pupils, e.g. Muslim dress code and daily prayer times.

(Male, 38, Tamworth)

The choice and freedom to choose the school and the education system appropriate to one's needs.

(Male, 47, Cambridge)

Good standard of education in an environment that is disciplined and caring, and that upholds moral values and standards, and is sensitive to individual needs and differences.

(Male, 57, Solihull)

My expectations would be that they support and fund the many excellent Islamic schools out there and help more to be set up. Indeed I'd like to see a day (soon I wish, but I guess I'm dreaming) more spaces that wanted by Muslims so that other children can benefit from these environments.

I would also like to see the state sector take a long hard look at the way it treats others. There was always a sense when I was at school that success at school meant learning to be 'white'. I find my friends with children in state schools saying that this still exists – there is still no sense of communities learning from each other, and more importantly a removal of this in-built arrogance from curriculums.

(Female, 34, London)

Islamic schools with an orientation to teach other faiths and incorporate diversity in full and be completely 'inclusive'.

(Male, 40, London)

Parents seemed inclined towards rapprochement within mainstream schooling as well as between mainstream schooling, identified generally as ideologically secular, and faith schooling. The demand for a middle path where Muslimness is respected in tangible ways across curricula and through-out educational cultures in Britain presents itself repeatedly as the ideal, with parents seeing a necessity for (and for the large part the only possibility of effecting) this duality and the 'mainstreaming' of Muslim faith schools supported by the state. Rather than representing a defensive segregation, parents saw these as a medium of transformation of children into higher-achieving, well-grounded individuals that can become confident members of society. As the correlations between experiences of discrimination and the preference for Muslim schools has already been investigated and some nuances teased out, these comments indicate that the preference bears the hallmark of challenge, rather than the negativity of reaction or disengagement (Ameli *et al.*, 2004).

In comparison, student respondents had a much more general set of expectations that focussed on the government facilitating positive images of Muslims through education and media, education of the educators, creating a better environment in terms of racial and religious equality as well as ecologically. Better teaching about other religions and improved awareness of Islam in the public realm as well as at schools was the biggest concern.

Students' expectations of the government had an overwhelming emphasis on the better teaching of religion in schools that encompasses Islam and other faiths. This combined with Muslim friendly facilities and codes as well as education of all teachers regarding Islam made up the bulk of recommendations. Again, whilst focusing on the mainstream, students are looking for Muslim education whereby their beliefs are respected, fairly represented across curricula and their Muslim identity facilitated. The experience of poor religious teaching or stereotyped imagery of Muslims permeating RE and other lessons is the realisation of the fears of Muslim parents, who often see Islamic faith schools as the only option to tackle these concerns:

> I expect the government to make greater effort to teach religious studies in schools by making it compulsory up to GCSE. I believe that there should also be more prayer rooms in schools to cater for Muslims.
>
> (Male, 17, London)

> My expectations of the Government are providing for more religious schools. Improving the environment by creating more recycling systems everywhere. Giving a wider view of different religions in all schools.
>
> (Female, 15, London)

> Improvements on the general environment and the way Muslims are portrayed in the media.
>
> (Female, 14, Wembley)

> Encouraging schools and universities to take students on academic merits rather than discriminating because of their faith or skin colour at interviews.
>
> (Female, 18, Brighton)

> I think the Government should intervene in providing people with a basic security whereby they can be safe from being discriminated against or bullied because of their faith. One way in which they could do this is to increase punishments to people who are offenders in this crime, so that it will deter people from committing this crime. The Government is a body that should enable everyone to have the same quality of life since they are representative of the whole country and so should therefore intervene in reducing the discrimination and bad experiences that Muslims are sometimes subject to.
>
> (Male, 15, London)

> I expect the government to educate the teachers as to the religion. Stop sensational journalism and use neutral language in rhetoric, i.e. not to target Muslims generally and indiscriminately.
>
> (Male, 17, Winchester)

My expectations of the government largely involve going more into the differences and details amongst Muslims and our teachings in schools, rather than glossing over the main points, such as the 'five pillars', and leaving it at that. It would be nice if more of the reasoning behind a few of Islam's more notorious teachings was explained, to make it clear to students that Islam is not a single minded, oppressive, violent religion, for example, the issue of women's rights in Islam.

University opportunities could also be improved, particularly at Oxford and Cambridge, for deserving Muslim students, to make us feel that we have more of a chance of getting in, and more of a reason to work for it, rather than being doubtful of the possibility of fulfilling our ambitions, whatever our ability.

(Male, 15, Middlesex)

More Islamic teachers. Prayer room. Special toilets.

(Female, 16, Wembley and Female, 15, Wembley)

Teachers being more educated in Islam.

(Male, Wembley)

Halal food served in catering.

(Female, London)

Teach people more about Islamic faith.

(Male, 15, London)

More positive images and not just bad things about Islam.

(Male, 12, London)

More talking about Islam.

(Female, 14, Wembley)

Improve the teaching of Islam in school

(Male, 16, London)

Teach lessons on Islam.

(Female, 17, London)

I think they should improve the R.E. teaching, they should bring forward new ideas about religion from the different schools of thought.

(Female, 14, East Sussex)

Give me choices, improve the scope of learning, make people improve their knowledge of other religions.

(Male, 16, Brighton)

Educate people to know more about Islam and the reality.

(Female, 15, London)

I expect the government to try and help remove the misconceptions of the Muslims that the general public have.

(Female, 18, Luton)

The government needs to create a society that treats everyone equally and a society that doesn't keep giving Muslims a negative label.

(Female, Luton)

Opportunities to educate the public as well as children about the values of Islam, explaining that hijab is no more threatening as is a nun's covering.

(Female, Luton)

Students appear more hopeful that with concerted action from the government the mainstream will become a less alienating space or conflictual base for them. Both options require the creation of Muslim educational space – where Islam is taught and respected and its adherents valued. Whilst parents – perhaps based on their own negative experiences – see Islamic schools as an ideal in the main, there is significant support amongst parents and students for a systemic change in educational spaces in the UK.

Interestingly, many students focused on the media as problem in the creation of stereotypes about Muslims, which they wanted, indeed expected, the government to deal with:

Improvements on the general environment and the way Muslims are portrayed in the media.

(Female, 14, Wembley)

Stop sensational journalism and use neutral language in rhetoric, i.e. not to target Muslims generally and indiscriminately.

(Male, 17, Winchester)

Put a stop on negative coverage in the media, which shows Islam as terrorism.

(Female, Luton)

The only thing that needs to be targeted is Islamophobia in media as that may have a negative effect in the future.

(Female, 17, Wembley)

This is a particularly interesting response in that it was not broached by any of the questions and is peculiar to the student group and is reflected nationally.

As discussed, creating a better environment was a repeated expectation, as were the provision of Muslim friendly facilities as well as a greater desire by government to listen to Muslims and respect them.

Putting more effort into creating environments where students can relate to each other in a more positive manner.

(Male, 17, Oldham)

They should give us our freedom to wear appropriate hijab in schools.

(Female, 19, Brighton)

More Islamic schools and more respect for Muslims.

(Female, 14, London)

Improving general environment.

(Female, 18, London)

They need to listen to Muslims more.

(Male, 18, Westminster)

Catering – halal.

(Male, London)

Teach Arabic.

(Male, 15, London)

Improving general environment.

(Female, 17, London)

Try getting rid of racial abuse.

(Male, 15, London)

COMMENTS FROM MUSLIM COMMUNITY FIGURES

IHRC asked a number of Muslim educationalists, teachers, activists and students for their response as to what they expect the government to do for Muslim students.

DR SHAIKH ABDUL MABUD,
DIRECTOR GENERAL, THE ISLAMIC ACADEMY, CAMBRIDGE

As Britain becomes increasingly multicultural, the education system should change to accommodate these various cultures and religions in order to allow children from minority groups to achieve their full potential and become valuable members of their own community and the country as a whole.

With around half a million Muslim children between the ages of 5-16 years being educated in mainstream British schools it is essential that specific educational needs are recognised and catered for by LEAs and schools. This is especially important in areas that are a source of concern for Muslim parents and their community, such as collective worship, religious education, sex education, school meals, mixed PE, some parts of the National Curriculum, etc. Schools should work with the Muslim community to inform parents of their rights in educating their children, including the rights of withdrawal from certain aspects of the National Curriculum. Teachers should also respect parents' decision to exercise this right and allow them to do so without any judgmental opinion.

In predominantly Muslim areas, religious subjects should be flexible and allow more detailed study of their own religion rather than predominantly Christianity.

In addition to creating more state-funded Muslim schools, where Muslim pupils are able to study National Curriculum subjects in a culturally enriching environment, opportunities should be created for *all* minority children in the mainstream system, through changes at the policy level, for them to engage with all aspects of school life, as valued members of society.

As Muslim pupils are underachieving educationally, this results in higher rates of unemployment in this group. It is vital that the reasons for such low achievement are explored and appropriate steps taken on a local and national level to rectify the situation. This includes involving Muslim parents and experts in order to help these children achieve their full potential, as doing so will allow a substantial part of the population to contribute positively as part of the workforce.

The problem of discrimination in schools must also be addressed, and the personal right of pupils to freely practise their religion granted by both teachers and fellow students. Pupils should be reassured of complete support of their teachers in any such instances.

At a deeper level all these require a change of attitude on the part of those who are responsible for both developing the curriculum and delivering it, without which a proper school ethos cannot be created where Muslim pupils can feel themselves as an integral part of school and indeed the wider society.

AMINA AL-YASSIN,
A-LEVEL STUDENT, LONDON

In the past, Islamic schools have been criticised for many different things – producing social outcasts, increasing divisions in society and instilling anti-citizenship values in its pupils and graduates. To the people who cast such allegations I ask – which Islamic school have you visited? To which of its pupils have you spoken? Because, to me, as a graduate of such an establishment, who then moved to a state funded grammar school and is soon to start a degree at Cambridge university – such accusations are completely unfounded and baseless.

The opponents of religious schools mainly argue that they are not representatives of society and therefore do not prepare individuals for "life in the real world" in the best possible way. If this argument were to be followed then all schools that do not represent society, including grammar and private schools, should be abolished. The aim of education in this country is to produce skilled and well-qualified citizens who are able to contribute to society and lead to its progress and betterment. Considering that much research has proven that this is more effectively achieved if people study in places where they are less likely to be attacked or harassed, then why not study in such places?

Starting at a new, non-Islamic, school was not as difficult as I had expected. Having been free to develop my ideas and opinions over the period of ten years at my old school, I found that I was confident enough in myself and reassured enough in my beliefs to anticipate all the challenges that lay ahead of me. Islamic teachings place much emphasis on the importance of cooperation, friendliness and integration. Pupils who have been taught in Islamic schools are more likely to have absorbed these values. The result is a well-rounded pupil who displays none of the qualities so feared by those who criticise religious schooling.

In my current school, girls who were previously educated in Islamic institutions have played an active role in all aspects of school life. They have become heads of the school sports team, been elected as school councillors, run the environmental campaigns and won prestigious awards and competitions. None of them felt that their previous educational environment had hindered them in any way.

One difference I have noted between Muslim girls educated in Islamic schools and those educated in mainstream ones is their willingness and desire to educate others about their beliefs and values. When twenty of us started at this new school together in September, we knew that we might be an odd sight – particularly as the number of practising Muslims at the school had been very low beforehand. Instead of keeping to ourselves, we sought to raise awareness about our culture and religion. Our Islamic society is very successful and has given assemblies, organised talks and even delivered R.E. lessons. More notably though, the Islamic society was the first religious society to organise a multi-faith event which was well attended by followers of many religions. It is when one realises just how much effort we put into bringing different people together that one can appreciate how hurt and offended we must have felt when we were asked whether we were planning the next terrorist attack in the prayer room.

What I believe this shows is that it is not religious schools that are the problem. If anything, they encourage feelings of brotherhood, love and tolerance in their pupils. The students that leave them move on to achieve many things, fuelled by the love for humanity that was instilled in them whilst in their

Islamic school. The problem is when pupils are not taught to appreciate other cultures and religions, and when one knows nothing about anyone else and the media is all they have to go by, it is no surprise that such offending remarks are made.

It is easy to demand the full integration of society – but the truth often is that Muslims are often left out whilst all the "integrating" goes on. Until more effort is put into educating people about their differences and teaching them to appreciate and celebrate them, Muslim pupils will continue being taught in their own schools. For, in the words of Diane Abbott, "when push comes to shove, everyone wants the best for their children".

RIYAZ DAYA,
24, ELSTREE, HERTS, CITY TRADER FORMERLY AT PRIVATE SCHOOL, FOLLOWED BY UNIVERSITY

The most striking disappointment that springs to mind when I recall my school days was the sheer inadequate nature of Religious and Social Studies. Apart from Christianity, no other religion was explored in any real detail. For example, with Islam there was very limited discussion of the different forms of Islam and the diverse nature of the cultures within which it is practised. In particular the association of violence with Islam was never really addressed and there was no exploration of the various causes of discontent within Muslim communities. This would help dispel many myths surrounding Islam and combat prejudice allowing Muslims to integrate further into British society.

On a related point, there was also an absence of any form of compulsory citizenship education. Civil empowerment is essential in order for a democracy to thrive, and courses in basic human rights, civil rights and political philosophy would help dispel social exclusion among a variety of minority communities.

JAMILA FERNANDEZ,
HEAD-TEACHER, THE AVENUE SCHOOL, LONDON

If one studies past and contemporary societies, it is clear that religion and education have strong and interconnected links. In the past, learning flourished in such places as mosques, temples and monasteries. Sacred books, scrolls and writings were used as the teaching resources. Unfortunately, when religious thinking becomes inward looking and intolerant of differing interpretations, and philosophical thought discouraged, education becomes a tool of indoctrination and persecution. In contrast to this, beautiful buildings, architecture, literacy and art created by mankind to evidence a magnificent creator – a celebration of the gift of life combine intellectual and spiritual learning.

In this country, one only has to look at a list of schools in an LEA to find schools created by Christian groups– Roman Catholics, Anglicans, Methodists, Baptists and Evangelists. In addition, there are Quaker and Jewish schools and schools established by ancient craft or trade organisations originating from a charitable trust. Some of these schools were created centuries ago, many agreed to become controlled as a result of the 1944 Education Act – no doubt because of the need for additional government financial support for staffing and the maintenance of old buildings (nothing changes!).

It is sad that all modern British Governments appear to be embarrassed by this history, despite many middle class politicians being products of this system and selecting such traditional schools for the education of their own offspring.

The present Government elected with a manifesto of "education, education, education", who sought popularity through statements about greater parental choice, who promised a wider variety of schools i.e. Foundation, Community and Specialist Status, continues to ignore four crucial elements of education today:

A multi-faith/multicultural society contains a growing and diverse Muslim community that requires the opportunity to select Muslim faith schools, few exist!

The Government is not supporting Muslim schools established with donations and private funding which aspire to become highly effective faith schools.

To obtain finance from Central Government for Voluntary-Aided Status is a difficult and bureaucratic nightmare.

The Government pretends not to understand the correlation between low achievement of Asian/Asian or British-Pakistani heritage 16 year-olds, who are failing to achieve 5+ A*-C grades at GCSE in maintained schools. Such pupils find themselves in a school community where their cultural, but more importantly their religious, identity does not exist – resulting in low self-esteem and low motivation.

Muslims expect governments to recognise and act upon these injustices that exist both for Muslim parents and pupils. An acknowledgement of the valuable and irreplaceable contribution that religion has made to the education system that Britain is proud of today remains to be made. There is a growing world faith represented in Britain today whose schools can co-exist alongside other established educational institutions. Politicians do not appear to recognise this, many choose to view the variety of faith in education as a divisive element. Muslim communities expect equal, or at least proportional, funding, resourcing and recognition of equal opportunity for Muslim pupils.

Finally, history has demonstrated that when man does not have the freedom to express himself spiritually in a society of religious tolerance and respect, moral behaviour declines and the world experiences man's inhumanity to man!

IBRAHIM HEWITT,
HEAD TEACHER, AL-AQSA PRIMARY SCHOOL, LEICESTER.

One in 10 state schools are in 'special measures', and children of Pakistani and Bangladeshi origin are performing academically worst of all… and the government's Chief Inspector of Schools appears to blame it all on independent Muslim schools in his 2004 annual report. Especially when it is Islam, faith is the forbidden f-word in education. I'm just waiting for some lunatic neo-con to blame Muslim schools for 9/11.

The National Curriculum leaves little room for cultural and religious sensitivity, while religious education is all too often tokenistic and unsatisfactory. Teacher training largely ignores religion so teachers are unprepared for working in multicultural schools. The results are shameful: after three decades of 'multi-faith' RE, ignorance about all faiths abounds, with intellectual and physical yobbery against Muslims in particular its inevitable result. Schools are expected to deliver one politically-inspired initiative after another, blamed when they don't work while exam results are massaged to demonstrate year-on-year growth, satisfying the politicians and justifying their policies. Teachers should be left to do what most do best – teach, and schools should be given greater autonomy for curriculum development that is best suited to the pupils in their care. Teach young Muslims to practise their faith and you will get good citizens. The 'one size fits all' approach doesn't work for adults; why should it work for children?

CHANGEZ ALI KHAN,
21, LAW STUDENT, BOLTON, LANCS

Spending seven years as a Muslim was generally a pleasant experience. Staff were very accommodating and made much effort to ensure that Muslim students were not left out of school life. We were able to obtain prayer facilities (at break time) on request from the Headmaster; for the purposes of dissection in Biology, horse hearts were provided instead of pig hearts for Muslim students; there was the option to eat vegetarian meals at school dinner; and, exceptionally, Muslim and Sikh students were permitted to wear beards on written request from their parents. I attended a fee-paying, boys'-only Protestant school and I think that such practices should be implemented in all state schools.

My only reservations about my school experience would concern obligatory hymn singing in music lessons (first and second years only); and RE lessons, which were only available during the first three years and which followed a very narrow syllabus (very little time spent on non-Christian beliefs). I feel that more of an effort should be made to encourage open dialogue between young people of different faiths: the classroom, under the supervision of the teacher, would provide an excellent arena.

HAJIRA QURESIHI,
20, MATHS STUDENT AT UNIVERSITY, FORMERLY
GRAMMAR SCHOOL STUDENT, SLOUGH, BERKS

Muslim students' expectation of the government is simple: to identify the concerns of Muslim students at schools and to take steps to help schools rectify the situations which are causing these concerns.

It should be understood by the government and schools that if they inhibit students in the areas which they think are of the utmost importance, they will not perform to their full potential and their education will be hampered.

There are some areas of concern which are very fundamental to our faith and which cannot be "left at home", as sometimes suggested, simply because they are practised at all times, regardless of where one is. These areas include: dress, food and prayer.

As regards dress, wearing loose and covering clothing is very important. Thus we should be allowed to wear headscarves and long skirts or jilbabs – the colours of which can of course be specified by schools to match school uniform. Men and boys should be allowed to grow beards, kept tidy and neat of course. For Physical Education and Sports lessons, boys and girls should be allowed to cover themselves by wearing tracksuit bottoms and, as always, head scarves for the girls. Some lessons, for example, swimming or PE lessons could be held in segregated classes to allow full participation from all students.

There should be allowance for halal food or at least a clear mention of the ingredients used in school canteens, thereby allowing for cases such as gelatine in desserts and mixed use of oil in frying meat and chips to be noted. This is of course helpful for vegetarians as well. Currently, many children just do not eat in schools because they do not feel they can trust what they are eating is halal or suitable for vegetarians, thereby skipping a meal.

Five times a day prayer is fundamental to our faith and sometimes as many as three prayers fall in a school day! All schools should have a prayer room which Muslim students can visit during break times, lunches, free periods and after-school where they can offer their daily prayers. If the school cannot provide one itself, the students should be allowed to find or delegate from amongst themselves a 'khateeb' to lead the Friday prayers. The current situation is that students spend their lunch times finding secret or quiet places where there are no teachers to quickly offer their prayers. It is a tense situation and lunchtimes can become scenes out of an action movie for these students!

In these three areas most schools in the UK are deficient. There are two further issues I would like to mention. These are relevant to different schools to a more or less extent depending on the location of the school, the population which attend it, etc. These are discrimination/bullying and Religious Studies.

There should, of course, (and I know initiatives do exist for bullying in general) be measures against bullying especially in schools where Muslims (or indeed anyone else) are a minority. Children should be taught tolerance from a young age as they will be the adults of tomorrow: they should be taught that being different is being normal.

As part of this programme, all faiths, and not just Christianity or Buddhism, should be taught so that all students can learn to realise, discuss, celebrate and treat as normal peoples' different faiths and practices. In a multicultural society like ours, nobody should be allowed to live in ignorance – ignorance which all too often and easily descends into needless fear and intolerance.

There are many situations I could outline and say what schools "should" be doing in such and such a situation but the underlying principle which needs to be conveyed, for the benefit of followers of any faith, is that schools need to be flexible in their rules and they need to understand that no child will perform to his or her best if they are feeling uncomfortable, unhappy, inhibited or repressed.

CONCLUSION

Equitable access to funding has for a long time been a keystone of the Muslim school movement in England and Wales, as highlighted earlier, and thus far five out of over 111 schools have been given access to state funding since 1998. Conversely, in the Netherlands the idea of equity has been firmly established, and, at the theoretical level, funding on an equal basis with other schools has been legally provided since 1917 and is readily available for religious minorities (Walford, 2001). Furthermore, Dutch Muslim schools tend to receive more funding than the average school because they are eligible for an extra allowance as a school where a pupil is from an ethnic group or 'whose parents have not been educated beyond the pre-vocational level'.

What is remarkable about the growing literature on globalisation and education is that the role of religion is generally ignored. The fact that world-based religions such as Catholic Christianity and Islam are international power sources which have missions other than those of economic globalisation appears to be marginalised in the globalisation analyses and debates. Muslim schools and Islamic education are crucial in the contemporary struggle for the formation of young people and for the shaping of their consciousness. Muslim schools strive to renew a culture of spirituality, virtue and service to the common good in an increasingly materialist and individualistic global market. The existence of Muslim schools constitutes part of the religious critique of the secular, without which both culture and freedom would be diminished.

Ethnic origin statistics reveal that pupils from all Pakistani and Bangladeshi communities perform less well than other pupils at all stages of compulsory education. In 2000 only 29% of Pakistani and Bangladeshi pupils gained five or more GCSE grades A*-C. This is the lowest of any ethnic group and far below the national average of 49%. At the same time they are well represented proportionally in terms of entry to university, particularly in London and Scotland. Only 5% of Muslim pupils attend a Muslim school. The remaining 95% of Muslim pupils attend their local state school and can find themselves in schools that are segregated in practice.

A large number of young Muslims have retained their Muslim identity and faith and have not seen this as an obstacle to contributing and integrating positively into mainstream British society. Single-sex education continues to be a major aspiration for the Muslim community, which sees the phasing out of such schools as contrary to their interests.

From the responses in the quantitative survey, respondents who had attended Muslim schools had described themselves as having a good strong identity and found it easy to integrate into society. Those pupils had no problems integrating in their new schools or colleges; indeed they were successful and high flying. Pupils were encouraged to join classes and extra-curricular activities outside school so they met and worked with people from other genders, religions, nationalities, etc.

The thorny issue in granting voluntary-aided status to Muslim schools is that unlike other denominations, this new group is predominantly of a visible minority. Racial segregation, as well as religious apartheid, appears to contradict all of the government's rhetoric on fostering multiculturalism. The argument that giving voluntary-aided status to Muslim schools would create racial segregation is flawed in the light of the fact that such "all-black" schools are already a reality in contemporary Britain. The European Convention on Human Rights requires that the state shall respect the rights of parents to ensure education and teaching in conformity with their own religious and philosophical convictions.

Article 9 of the new Human Rights Act (1998) specifically refers to 'freedom of thought, conscience and religion' – entitlements, which could provide ample opportunities for use by ethnic minority and religious groups. According to Article 29 of the Convention on the Rights of the Child, the education of the child shall be directed to the development of respect for the child's parents, his or her cultural identity, language and values, the national values of the country in which the child is living, the country from which he or she may originate and civilisations different from his or her own.

Regarding the National Curriculum, Tomlinson (2001) quotes that it offers 'little change or guidance to the next generation of young people, on how to live together in conditions of mutual respect and equity' (p. 148). Tomlinson has also observed that Christian 'fundamentalism', perceived liberal freedoms and pseudo-democratic assertions have served to hide or disguise many other forms of social division, inequity and injustice. The differences are more realised when the freedom within Islam is actualised. The starting point in Islam is the development of a confident sense of self, yet within a supportive collective culture, built upon religious tenets.

During a visit to the Islamia school, Prince Charles paid a tribute saying :

"I really do believe that the Islamia school is an important model and it will be interesting to see how many more develop in the future.
You are ambassadors for a much misunderstood faith. You have much to tell people in a secular society like ours."[19]

Muslim schools are seen to act as a moral compass for the nation as a whole and provide a much better ethos than that which pertains in community schools. Whilst British society is generally becoming more secular, religion for many people is an organising principle and is an influential force in the shaping of contemporary Britain. Attempts to address inequalities must take place at both the socio-political (macro) and institutional (micro) levels if they are to permeate throughout.

Creating a 'Muslim educational space' – whether through Muslims schools or within the mainstream thus appears to be not only the desire of most Muslims, but a requirement if the British educational system is to truly cater for and include all sectors of society. 'Muslim' space in this regard means a multifaceted approach to not only respecting the faith of others and allowing it separate space to be nurtured, but including it within a wider space where it becomes normalised and taken for granted by those who do not profess it or indeed any other confession.

19

British Muslims Monthly Survey 2000 a, p. 1

This study has shown that whilst the experience of discrimination is high, and whilst there is a correlation between the desire for separate Muslim schools and experiences of discrimination, such a desire is not unique only to those who have such experiences, or indeed those who profess high religiosity. When assessed in terms of engendering a sense of inclusive citizenship, the findings of the survey, contextualised within the current debate and theory, show that: this space is seen to be necessary to the project of creating emotional attachment amongst minorities to the state; this space has already gone a long way towards fulfilling that with those professing high loyalty and sense of affiliation; and that those having less experience of discrimination consistently opt for the choice of Muslim school for their children.

These voices need to be heard and accommodated as a matter of urgency within a policy driven debate that equates religiosity – particularly Muslim religiosity – with hostility to ideas of inclusivity, loyalty and shared citizenship. This study in fact indicates that the converse is true, and the defining factors that make 'Muslim' educational space desirable for Muslims are actually desirable for all.

RECOMMENDATIONS TO THE GOVERNMENT

For young Muslims the education system is the earliest and the most significant point of contact with the wider community. The message that the education system provides, in respecting and accommodating their needs, will have a significant influence on their attitude to integration and participation in society. The vast majority of Muslims continue to be educated in non-Muslim state schools. Successful integration requires such schools to change to meet the legitimate expectations of Muslims in order to ensure the provision of equal rights by differential treatment. Without the acceptance and facilitation of these differences, there can be little genuine sense of civic community within educational spaces for children in the UK. Muslims in this context will remain excluded and held back in terms of acheivement by an education system that promotes narrow, aggressive and often hostile ideological ideas of education that simply alienate and demonise those it should nurture.

ACCOMMODATION OF RELIGIOUS NEEDS

Schools should as far as possible accommodate the religious needs of pupils. This includes facilitating uniforms that meet religious requirements, allowing beards for boys and hijab for girls, allowing prayer and the breaking of fasts. It also requires that schools accept that some aspects of its curricula are not compliant with the beliefs and practices of its Muslim students and that they should be allowed to defer from these without penalty, e.g. where Muslims object to music or dance lesson. Where their objections stem from issues surrounding mixed-sex PE or swimming, for example, the possibility of segregating should be seriously looked at as an option. Such reworking of curricula should not be seen as negative enterprises and student teachers need training as to the normative values of such exercises in the process of fostering equality.

The Court of Appeal ruling in the Shabina Begum case (March 2004) regarding the wearing of jilbab is an opportunity for the government to set guidelines that give clarity to the schools over their human rights obligations when setting uniform policies. The media hype that surrounds this case is one that the government needs to address through such a process to avoid the demonisation not just of Muslim students like Shabina Begum – as has happened – but also the processes of human rights reasoning that led to the Court of Appeal's decision. It is also important to create parity between minorities. Current anomalies in UK law mean that some minorities have full protection for their religious practices in the school environment whilst others – notably Muslims – have none.

Without the creation of a respectful culture of difference through the facilitation of religious needs within the mainstream, Muslim students and those of other minorities will never be able to meet the 'normative' requirements of existing school cultures.

USE FAITH IDENTITY TO RAISE ACHIEVEMENT

Ways should be found in which faith identities can be harnessed to improve educational standards among Muslim pupils. The sense of value and identity associated with faith is a repeated reason given by parents for their preference of Muslim faith schools. Research indicates, and results have shown, that Muslim faith schools (indeed faith schools generally) see higher than national and local average exam results. The complex of reasons as to why this is the case need to be examined and the lessons applied to mainstream schools, where most Muslim children are educated and will be for the fore-seeable future. If better educational results are a goal (as the increasingly per-formance obsessed educational culture indicates), and better education leads to more liberalisation in values as parts of this and other research has shown, utilising these benefits of faith identity within the mainstream seems logical. The role of faith identity within the mainstream needs to be destigmatised and evaluated as a tried and tested option that has a valuable lesson to impart at a systemic level across British education.

RADICALLY IMPROVE EDUCATION ABOUT ISLAM

There is a need to integrate education about Islam into the general schooling process, not least within the teaching of religion in RE/RS classes. The current situation, where formal, standardised, impartial training or even basic qualifications in the teaching of the subject are not required, has left the teaching of a subject crucial to the fostering of understanding between diverse pupils sets, to the biases and sometimes overtly discriminatory whims of teachers. Whether intentionally ill-meaning or simply unknowing vehicles of institutionalised prejudice, poorly trained RE/RS teachers are clearly not delivering an education about Islam that fosters respect of its adherents and norms. Whilst debate and disagreement should be encouraged, a culture of reason and respect needs to be injected into that process. Muslims' need for this recognition is a basic criteria for fulfilling a sense of belonging to the community. If this is not provided at school it will not be expected or indeed delivered outside, provoking and exacerbating both hostility against Muslims and exactly the withdrawal that has thus far not been evidenced despite much supposition of the same.

RELIGIOUS AWARENESS TRAINING FOR STAFF AND GOVERNORS SHOULD BE INSTITUTED AT NON-MUSLIM SCHOOLS

Pupils in particular reflected a desire for better understanding. The experience of subtle, unintentional but ultimately institutionalised Islamophobia through the purveyance of misconceptions about students has been a striking feature of this survey. Instances of overt bullying by staff and students alike is of course cause for concern in itself and government needs to take a hard look at the reality on the ground in the mainstream system before levelling attacks at faith schools.

BETTER TEACHER TRAINING ON DIVERSITY

Training should be provided for teachers regarding religious diversity and aspects of religions. The gap between the expectation of equal treatment from educators and the reality of the perpetuation of deeply held social prejudices is large and all too real with Muslim students. Where the law currently fails in protecting all religious minorities equally, other systems can and should try to incorporate rigorous and evolving diversity awareness. This awareness needs to be backed up with practical examples of how to place diversity within the teaching system of individual teachers as well as part of the general ethos of a school. Successes do exist, but these seem few and isolated exceptions to the general Islamophobic rule.

FUNDING FOR MUSLIM SCHOOLS

The state needs to be able to address the funding issues surrounding faith-based schools, allowing full movement to the state sector or partial funding through any of its funding structures, including freeing councils to fund existing or potential independent schools. In order to address concerns regarding the wastage of state funding as a result of the fear of interference in curricula on the part of Muslim schools, the government needs to find means of checking achievement in a non-invasive fashion.

Allowing existing Muslim schools to move into the state sector is a long overdue start to a process of mainstreaming Muslim education in line with other faiths. State funding of faith schools should not be seen as a formula for socially engineering minority communities through interference, but protecting minority rights and encouraging participatory citizenship.

Only by recognising Muslim parents' rights to choice, and equality in choice with other parents will Muslims as individuals and communities feel the sense of benefit of shared civic identities. Multiple loyalties – to faith, nation and beyond – need to be understood and harnessed as potential transformer of education for all in the UK. If Muslim parents are not afforded the right to instil a sense of who they are within their children in the manner they see best, there will be either disappointed and disaffected parents or demonised and often depressed children finding little incentive to participate in the wider society. To leave the situation as it is or advocate for a lessening role of faith schools or faith recognition in the mainstream augurs ill for participatory dynamics amongst minority communities such as the Muslim communities. To do nothing runs the risk of Muslims seeing this as the frustration of another legitimate aspiration.

TAX BREAKS SHOULD BE OFFERED FOR PARENTS WHO WISH TO EDUCATE THEIR CHILDREN AT HOME

Home schooling as an alternative to mainstream education is rapidly growing across the UK, and should be facilitated as a means of relieving pressure from the education system and also as a means of fostering choice. As an increasingly popular educational choice for parents, the government needs to provide meaningful support for those parents embarking on such a course.

THE NATIONAL CURRICULUM NEEDS TO REFLECT A BALANCE OF PERSPECTIVES, INCORPORATING THE ACHIEVEMENTS AND CONTRIBUTIONS OF CULTURAL GROUPS.

There should be an end to the simplistic "sarees and somosas" teaching of Muslim culture. The curriculum needs to place more emphasis on Muslim beliefs, practices and their history in Britain and their contribution to British society. This is an initiative that should look at the values and contributions of all minority groups in an inclusive manner. Without that level of validation, discussions about fostering citizenship within the mainstream has little meaning. Students need to feel they belong, and that they have a stake in a society that includes them and not at best tolerates them. This sense of emotional belonging can only be generated if at the system level of schools – their first interface with institutionalised society – they are considered peers in the process of social development through current and historical contribution.

Part of this means including as standard, the contribution of Muslims to science, maths and civilisation, and not portraying history in a one-sided view that ultimately reflects a British or European chauvinism.

GENERATING DIALOGUE THROUGH THE NATIONAL CURRICULUM

Modifying the National Curriculum to open up greater possibility of dialogue between different faith-based groups, in such as a way as to help break down the stereotypical assumptions between them and community schools, is a huge but necessary task.

Depicting Islam as an Abrahamic religion like Judaism and Christianity and not the "other" or "new" religion which was "influenced by the Judaeo-Christian traditions", is a necessary part of this process. This will help to de-Orientalise Islam and its adherents. Given the multi-ethnic make-up of Muslim society, particularly in the UK, this would also encourage broader and more inclusive thinking regarding other faiths from outside the Abrahamic tradition. Whilst discussions of faith bases have not completely eradicated racism within faith groups, they have gone some way towards this goal. The inclusivity afforded to Judaic tradition has been a significant marker in the struggle against anti-Semitism, and should be seriously considered as part of the struggle towards ending specifically Islamophobia. The encouraging of dual education for adherents of the Jewish faith has exemplary lessons for Muslim education in the UK. State support for Jewish faith schools, as well as provision for Jewish faith assemblies at schools, kosher meals, etc. are more commonplace and less controversial. The strengthening and the encouragement of this polycentrism that recognises shared and particular educational realms as a route to educational and civic success amongst other faiths is realistic. The staggeringly high emphasis placed on the teaching of religion by student respondents highlights a serious flaw within the mainstream education system that needs to be looked at in new and radical ways if we are to avoid alienating another generation of young Muslims.

BIBLIOGRAPHY

Addis, A. (1996) 'On human diversity and the limits of toleration' in I. Shapiro and W. Kymliicka (eds.) *Ethnicity and Group Rights*, New York, pp.112-153.

Ahmed, N. Bodi, F. Kazim R., & Shadjareh M. (2001) *The Oldham Riots: Discrimination, Deprivation and Communal Tension in the United Kingdom*, London, Islamic Human Rights Commission.

Akhtar, S. (1992) *White Paper on Muslim Education in Great Britain*, London, The Muslim Institute.

al Guindi, Fadwa (1999) *Veil: Modesty, Privacy and Resistance*, Oxford, Berg.

Ameli, S. R. & Merali, A. (2004) *Dual Citizenship: British, Islamic or Both? Obligation, Recognition, Respect and Belonging*, London, Islamic Human Rights Commission.

Ameli, S. R., Elahi, M., & Merali A. (2004) *Social Discrimination: Across the Muslim Divide*, London, Islamic Human Rights Commission.

Ansari, H. (2004) *The Infidel From Within*, London, C. Hurst & Co.

Anwar, M. (1996), *British Pakistanis; Demographic, Social and Economic Position*, Coventry, Centre for Research in Ethnic Relations: University of Warwick.

Anwar, M. (1979) *Myth of Return: Pakistanis in Britain*, London, Heinemann

Armstrong, K. (2000) *The Battle for God: Fundamentalism in Judaism, Christianity and Islam*, London, Harper Collins

Arthur, J. (1995) 'Government Education Policy and Voluntary-aided Schools', *Oxford Review of Education,* Vol. 21, No. 4, pp. 447–455.

Ashraf, S. A. & Hussain, S. S. (1979) *Crisis in Muslim Education*, Jeddah, Hodder & Stoughton and King Abdulaziz University.

Banks, J. A., *et al.* (1997) *World: Adventures in Time and Place*, New York, Macmillan McGraw-Hill.

BBC News/Education; 2/6/02; 6/30/03; 9/11/03.

Bednarz, S. *et al.* (1997) *Discover Our Heritage*, Boston, Houghton Muffin.

Bell, David (2005) 'What does it mean to be a citizen?' speech to the Hansrad Society reprinted at:

http://education.guardian.co.uk/faithschools/story/0,13882,1392281,00.html

Berger, P. (1973) *The Social Reality of Religion*, London, Penguin.

Blair, M. (2001) 'The Education of Black Children: Why Do Some Schools Do Better Than Others?' in R. Majors (ed.) *Educating Our Black Children*, London, Routledge Falmer.

British Muslims Monthly Survey May 2000, Vol. VIII, No. 5.

British Muslims Monthly Survey September 2001, Vol. IX, No 9.

British Muslims Monthly Survey, February 2002, Vol. X, No. 2.

British Muslims Monthly Survey March 2002 Vol. X, No. 3.

British Muslims Monthly Survey May 2002 Vol. X, No. 5.

Cashmore, E. & Jennings, J. eds. (2001) *Racism: Essential Readings,* London, Sage.

Carmichael, S. & Hamilton, C. V. (1967) *Black Power: The Politics of Liberation in America,* London, Penguin.

Cline, T. & Shamsi, S. (2000) *Language Needs or Special Needs? The Assessment of Learning Difficulties in Literacy Among Children Learning English as an Additional Language: a Literature Review*, London, DFEE.

Commission for Racial Equality (1988) *Learning in Terror: Survey of Racial Harassment in Schools and Colleges,* Commission For Racial Equality (CRE)

Convention on the Rights of the Child, 1989, 44/25, annex, 44 UN GAOR

Dawkins, Richard (2001) 'Children must choose their own beliefs' *The Observer,* December 30.

Department for Education & Skills (DFES) (2001) *Schools Achieveing Success: Consultation on Education White Paper.*

Department for Education & Skills (DFES) (2003a) *Youth Co-Horts Study: The Activities and Experiences of 16 year-olds: England & Wales* SFR 04/2003, London, DFES.

Donald, J. & Rattansi, A. (1992), *'Race', Culture and Difference.* London: Sage.

Douglass, S. L. & Dunn, R. E. (2001) 'Interpreting Islam in American schools', in H. Donnan (ed.), *Interpreting Islam*, pp. 76–98, London, Sage Publications.

Durkheim, E. (1971) *The Elementary Form of the Religious Life: a study in Religious Sociology,* London, Allen and Unwin.

Dwyer, C. & Meyer, A. (1995) 'The institutionalisation of Islam in the Netherlands and in the UK: the case of Islamic schools', *New Community* 21 : 37–54.

Eade, J. and Zaman, F. (1997) *Routes and Beyond: Voices From Educationally Successful Bangladeshis*, London, Centre for Bangladeshi Studies. *Education Reform Act* 1988, HMSO.

Eggleston, S. J., Dunn, D. K., Anjali, J. M., & Wright, C. (1986) *Education for Some: The Educational & Vocational Experiences of 15 – 18 year-old Members of Minority Ethnic Groups*, Trentham, Stroke on Trent.

Epstein, D., Elwood, J., Hey, V., & Maw, J. (eds.) (1998) *Failing Boys? Issues in Gender and Achievement*, Florence, KY: Taylor & Francis.

Esposito, J. (1995) *The Islamic Threat : Myth or Reality?* New York, Oxford University Press.

'Faith as the basis of education in a multi-faith multi-cultural country: A discussion document', (based on joint seminar of The Islamic Academy, Cambridge and the Department of Education, University of Cambridge), (1990) The Islamic Academy, Cambridge.

Feheney, M. (ed.) (1998*) From Ideal to Action: the inner nature of a Catholic school today*, Dublin, Veritas.

Fetzer J. S. & Soper J. C. (2003) *The Roots of Public Attitudes Toward State Accommodation of European Muslims' Religious Practices Before and After September 11*, London, Blackwell Publishing.

Gallagher, M. P. (1997) 'New Forms of Cultural Unbelief' in P. Hogan and K. Williams (eds.), *The Future of Religion in Irish Education*, Dublin, Veritas.

Gillborn, D. (2000) 'Anti-Racism: from Policy to Praxis', in Bob Moon, Sally Brown and Miriam Ben-Peretz (eds.), *Routledge International Companion to Education*, pp. 476–488, London, Routledge.

Gillborn, D. & Gipps, C. (1996) *Recent Research on the Achievements of Ethnic Minority Pupils*, Report for the Office for Standards in Education, London, HMSO.

Gillborn, D. & Mirza, H. S. (2000) *Educational Inequality: Mapping Race, Class and Gender—A Synthesis of Research Evidence*, Report #HMI 232, London, Office for Standards in Education.

Gillborn, D. & Youdell, D. (2000) *Rationing Education: Policy, Practice, Reform and Equity,* Buckingham, Open University Press.

Gillborn, D. (2004) 'Racism, Policy and Contemporary Schooling : Current Inequities and Future Possibilities' *SAGE Race Relations Abstracts* 29: 5-33.'

Gordon P. & Klug, F. (1986) *New Right New Racism*, London, Searchlight.

Grace, G. (2002) *Catholic Schools*, p. 14, London, Routledge Falmer.

Grace, G. (1998) 'Critical policy scholarship: Reflections on the integrity of knowledge and research', in G. Shacklock & J. Smith (eds.), *Being Reflexive in Critical Education and Social Research*, London, Falmer Press.

Grace, G. (1998b) 'The future of the Catholic school: an English perspective', in Feheney, J. (ed.), *From Ideal to Action: the inner nature of a Catholic school today*, Dublin, Veritas.

Grinter, R. 'Transferring the National Curriculum Developments in an Antiracist Campaign', *Multicultural Teaching*, 8, 3, Summer 1990, p. 26

Gunder-Frank, A. and Gills, B. (1992) 'The Five Thousand Year Old System: An Interdisciplinary Introduction', *Humboldt Journal of Social Relations* Vol 18 (1).

Hallam, S. (2002) 'Ability Grouping in Schools', *Perspectives on Education Policy*, No. 13, London, Institute of Education: University of London.

Hallam, S. & Toutounji, I. (1996) *What Do We Know About the Grouping of Pupils by Ability? A Research Review*, London, University of London Institute of Education.

Halstead, M. (1993) 'Educating Muslim Minorities: Some Western European Approaches', in W. Tulaisiewicz and Ch. To (eds.), *World Religions and Educational Practice*, London, Cassell.

Hanes, W. T. III (ed.) (1997) *World History : Continuity and Change*, Austin, TX: Holt, Reinhart and Winston.

Haynes, C. C. & Thomas, O. (eds.) (1994) *Finding Common Ground*, Nashville, TN: Freedom Forum First Amendment Center, Vanderbilt University.

Hewer, C. (1992) 'Muslim Teacher Training in Britain', *Muslim Education Quarterly*, Vol. 9, No. 2, pp. 21–34, The islamic Academy, Cambridge.

Hewer, C. (2001) 'Schools for Muslims', *Oxford Review of Education*, Vol. 27, No 4.

Home Office; *Home Office Code of Practice on Reporting and Recording Racist Incidents*, (April 2000): 16.
Human Rights Act (1998), Her Majesty's Stationery Office
Islamophobia: A Challenge for Us All (1997) London,
Runnymede Trust.

Kemp, S. and Gillborn, D. (2000) *Achievement in Southwark: A Qualitative Study*, Presentation at the Southwark Teachers' Centre, London Borough of Southwark, 1 December.

Krieger, L. S., Neill, K. & Jantzen, S. L. (1997) *World History: Perspectives on the Past*, Lexington, MA : D.C. Heath.

Lodge, B. (1991) 'Curriculum Council Is 'Too Secular'', *Times Educational Supplement*, 20 September, p. 11.

Mabud, S. A. (1992) 'A Muslim Response to the Education Reform Act of 1988', *British Journal of Religious Education*, Vol. 14, pp. 88–98.

Macpherson, W. (1999) *The Stephen Lawrence Inquiry*, Cm 4262–I, London, The Stationery Office

Marquand, D. (1988) 'The Paradoxes of Thatcherism', in R. Skidelsky (ed.) *Thatcherism*, Chatto & Windus.

McLaughlin, T. (1990) *Parental Rights in Religious Upbringing and Religious Education within a Liberal Perspective*, PhD Thesis, University of London.

Miller, H. (2001) 'Meeting the Challenges: the Jewish schooling phenomenon in the UK', *Oxford Review of Education*, Vol. 27, No. 4, pp. 501–513.

Modood, T. (1994) 'Establishment, multiculturalism and British citizenship.' *Political Quarterly*, 65(1), p. 71.

Modood, T. & Werbner, P. (1997) *The Politics of Multiculturalism in the New Europe: Racism, Identity and Community*, London, Zed Books.

Molokotos-Liederman, L. (2000) 'Religious Diversity in Schools: The Muslim Headscarf Controversy & Beyond', *Social Compass*, 47(3), pp. 367–381.

Morris, A. B. (1998a) "Catholic and other secondary schools: an analysis of OFSTED inspection reports', 1993-1995, *Educational Research*, Vol. 40, No.2, pp. 181–190.

Morris, A. B. (1998b) 'So far, so good: levels of academic achievement in Catholic schools', *Educational Studies*, 24, 1, pp. 83–94.

Natural History Museum Publications *Man's Place in Evolution*, 1981, Cambridge, Cambridge University Press,

Newbigin, L., Sanneh, L., & Taylor, J. (eds.) (1998) *The Secular Myth*, London, SPCK.

Oakes, J. (1990) *Multiplying Inequalities: The Effects of Race, Social Class, and Tracking on Opportunities to Learn Mathematics and Scienc*e, Santa Monica, CA: The Rand Corporation.

Office for Standards in Education (Ofsted) (1996) *Exclusions from Secondary Schools* for Standards in Education (Ofsted) (1999) *Raising the Attainment of Minority Ethnic Pupils*, London, Ofsted.

Office for Standards in Education (Ofsted) (2001) *Improving Attendance and Behaviour in Secondary Schools,* London, Ofsted.

Office for National Statistics (ONS) (2001) *2001 Census*, London, ONS. Available at: http://www.ons.gov.uk/census2001

Ouseley, Herman (2001) *Community Pride not Prejudice:Making Diversity Work in Bradford* Bradford, Bradford Vision

Parekh, B. (2000) *Rethinking Multiculturalism: Cultural Diversity and Political Theory*, Basingstoke, Macmillan Press.

Parekh, B. *et al.* (2000) *The Future of Multi-Ethnic Britain,* London, Profile Books.

Parker-Jenkins, M. & Hartas, D. (2000) 'Child Rearing Practices : A Cross Cultural Perspective', in A. A. Hosin (ed.), *Issues in Applied Developmental Psychology and Child Psychiatry,* Lampeter, Wales, Edwin Mellen Press.

Parker-Jenkins, M., Hartas, D., & Irving, B. (2005) *In Good Faith: Schools, Religion and Public Funding*, Aldershot, Hants: Ashgate.

Patterson, S. (1969) *Immigration and Race Relations in Britain, 1960–1967,* London, Oxford University Press.

Pearson, Alison 'Maybe Muslim parents are right after all, Mr Bell', *Evening Standard*, Wednesday 19th January 2005

'Pros and cons of faith schools' Hard Talk, BBC, 6 February 2002, http://news.bbc.co.uk/1/hi/education/1804427.stm

Randall, S. (1998) 'The New Right: Racism and Education in Thatcher's Britain', *Sage Race Relations Abstracts*, 13, 3, August, pp. 3–17.

Sawar, G. (1994) *British Muslims and Schools*, London, Muslim Educational Trust.

Schutz, A (1971) Collected Papers Vol. 1: *The Problem of Social Reality,* The Hague: Martinus Nijhoff.

Scott-Baumann, A. (2003) 'Teacher Education for Muslim Women: Intercultural Relationships, Method and Philosophy', *Ethnicites*, 3, pp. 243–261.

Sewell, T. (1998) 'Loose Canons: Exploding the Myth of the 'Black Macho' Lad', in D. Epstein *et al.* (eds.) *Failing Boys? Issues in Gender and Achievement*, pp. 111–127, Buckingham, Open University Press.

Smith D. J. & Tomlinson, S. (1989) *The School Effect: A Study of Multi Racial Comprehensives,* London, Policy Studies Institute.

Sukhnandan, L. & Lee, B. (1998) *Streaming, Setting and Grouping by Ability*, Slough, Educational Research.

Swann, Lord (1985) *Education for All: Final Report of the Committee of Inquiry into the Education of Children from Ethnic Minority Group*s, Cmnd 9453, London: HMSO.

Sylvester, Rachel (2001)'Morris attacks church schools ' 08/09, *Daily Telegraph*

Tamney, J. B. (1992a) *The Resilience of Christianity in the Modern World,* Albany, NY: State University of New York Press.

Tamney. J. B. (1994) *Conservative Government and Support for the Religious Institution: Religious Education in English Schools.* The British Journal of Sociology, Vol. 45 (2), pp. 195.

Taylor, M. J. & Hegarty, S. (1985) *The Best of Both Worlds? A Review of Research into the Education of Pupils of South Asian Origin,* Windsor, NFER-Nelson.

Times Eduactional Supplement, (1998) 'Muslims gain equality to funding' 16th January, p. 18.

Thatcher, M. (1988) 'Speech to General Assembly of the Church of Scotland', Margaret Thatcher Foundation http://www.margaret-thatcher.org/speeches/displaydocument.asp?docid=107246.

Thatcher, M. (1993) *The Downing Street Years,* London, Harper Collins.

Tomlinson, S. (1987) 'Curriculum Option Choices in Multi-Ethnic Schools', in B. Troyna (ed.), *Racial Inequality in Education,* pp. 105–106.

Tomlinson, S. (2001) *Education in Post-welfare Society,* Buckingham, Open University Press

Townsend, H. & Brittan, E. (1972) *Organization in Multiracial Schools,* National Foundation for Educational Research.

Troyna, B. (ed.) (1987) *Racial Inequality in Education,* pp.105–106, London, Hutchinson.

Troyna, B. & Siraj-Blatchford, I. (1993) 'Providing Support or Denying Access? The Experiences of Students Designated as 'ESL' and 'SN' in a Multi-Ethnic Secondary School', *Educational Review,* 45 (1), pp. 3 – 11.

Walford, Geoffrey (2001) 'Funding for religious schools in England and the Netherlands. Can the piper call the tune? *Research Papers in Education,* 16, 4, pp. 359-380

Wallbank, T. W., *et al.* (1987) *History and Life: The World and Its People,* 3rd Ed, Glenview, IL: Scott Foresman.

Warren, S. & Gillborn, D. (2003) *Race Equality and Education in Birmingham,* Birmingham: Birmingham City Council and Birmingham Race Action Partnership.

Weller, P., Feldman, A. & Purdham, K. (2001) *Religious Discrimination in England and Wales: Interim Report,* London, Home Office.

Wright, C., Weekes, D. & McGlaughlin, A. (2000) *"Race", Class and Gender in Exclusion from School,* London, Falmer. Universal Declaration of Human Rights (1948)